ALEXANDER THE GREAT
CONQUEROR OF THE KNOWN WORLD

Don Nardo

MORGAN REYNOLDS
PUBLISHING

Alexander the Great: Conqueror of the Known World

Copyright © 2010 by Morgan Reynolds Publishing

Library of Congress Cataloging-in-Publication Data

Nardo, Don, 1947-
 Alexander the Great : conqueror of the known world / contents by Don Nardo. – 1st ed.
            p.   cm.
 Includes bibliographical references and index.
 ISBN 978-1-59935-126-1 (alk. paper)
 1.   Alexander, the Great, 356-323 B.C.—Juvenile literature. 2.   Greece—History—Macedonian Expansion, 359-323 B.C.—Juvenile literature. 3.   Generals—Greece—Biography—Juvenile literature. 4.   Greece—Kings and rulers—Biography—Juvenile literature. I. Title.
 DF234.N37 2009
 938'.07092—dc22
 [B]
                                2009019641

Printed in the United States of America
First edition

CONTENTS

A sculpture from the fourth century BC depicting Alexander on horseback
(*Courtesy of Erich Lessing/Art Resources*)

CHAPTER ONE

THE WORLD OF ALEXANDER'S BOYHOOD

When the man history calls Alexander the Great was born, civilization was already immensely ancient. Far to the east of his homeland, the Greek kingdom of Macedonia, lay the wide plains of Mesopotamia (what is now Iraq). There, thousands of years before Alexander's time, the practice of agriculture had first begun. The world's first cities had risen from the region's fertile plains, and humanity's first writing systems had been invented within their walls. Meanwhile, in Egypt, hundreds of miles south of Greece great ages of empire and culture elapsed before Alexander drew his first breath. Indeed, nearly the same amount of time separated Alexander from the building of Egypt's towering pyramid-tombs as separates the present day from Alexander.

Many powerful rulers and successful conquerors had come and gone in those vast ages prior to Alexander. The names of some—like Sargon, Hammurabi, Ramses, and Pericles—are well known today. Yet in the eye of history, their deeds pale in comparison to his. While still in his twenties, Alexander, by then Macedonia's king,

A second-century BC medallion of Alexander the Great

The Fury of Achilles (1737) by French painter Charles Antoine Coypel

proved himself an enormously resourceful ruler as well as a military general of uncanny skill. And before his untimely death at age thirty-three, he carved out the largest empire the world had ever seen. Moreover, long after his passing almost every ambitious ruler measured his own accomplishments using Alexander as a yardstick. A story has survived about the famous Roman general Julius Caesar beholding a statue of the renowned Macedonian. Caesar is said to have expressed deep regret that by age thirty-one he had achieved little, whereas by that age Alexander had captured much of the known world.

Similarly, Alexander embraced his own personal hero: Achilles. Achilles was the central character of the *Iliad,* an epic poem by the Greek poet Homer, who lived some five centuries before Alexander. It tells the story of the final year of the legendary Trojan War. In it, Achilles, a nearly invincible warrior, dies young after spectacular achievement and glory.

Alexander came to believe that, like his hero, he too was fated to accomplish deeds that all future ages would remember. And for that singular opportunity he was prepared to pay the price of his life. According to Alexander's principal ancient biographer, Arrian, he told his soldiers: "Those who endure hardship and danger are the ones who achieve glory; and the most gratifying thing is to live with courage and to die leaving behind eternal renown." As a result, there was a perpetual sense of urgency about nearly everything Alexander did. It was as if he had to make his indelible mark on history before time ran out. This peculiar vision of mortality and greatness seems to have been one of the chief motivating forces of his short but eventful life.

It is important to note that this aura of destiny that came to surround Alexander and his deeds materialized only after he had made a reputation as a talented and ruthless conqueror. There was little in his family's or nation's background to suggest that either would ever produce an individual of his enormous achievement.

True, ancient stories have survived containing prophecies about his special, even miraculous birth. It was said that holy men told his father, King Philip II, that the baby would grow into an adult who would be invincible. And another prophecy said that at the time of Alexander's birth, the temple of the goddess Artemis would be destroyed by fire—it was in fact burned by an arsonist seeking fame. (Located in the Greek city Ephesus, in Asia Minor, what is now Turkey, it was later listed among the seven wonders of the ancient world.) A different birth prophecy was recorded by another of Alexander's ancient biographers, Plutarch:

> The bride [Alexander's mother, Olympias] dreamed that there was a crash of thunder, that her womb was struck by a thunderbolt, and that there followed a blinding flash from which a great sheet of flame blazed up and spread far and wide before it finally died away. Then, sometime after their marriage, Philip saw himself in a dream in the act of sealing up his wife's womb and [beheld], so it seemed to him, the figure of a lion. . . .[Thereafter, a fortune-teller predicted that Olympias] would bring forth a son whose nature would be bold and lion-like.

However, there is no reason to believe that any of these predictions were made before or at the time Alexander was born in 356 BC. Modern scholars believe that they were fabricated when he was already grown and/ or following his death. In fact, such omens (divine signs) and legends of miraculous births grew up about most ancient figures who became powerful,

ALEXANDER'S ANCIENT BIOGRAPHERS

Plutarch
*(Courtesy
StockImages/
Alamy)*

The accounts penned by Arrian and Plutarch are among the five principal ancient sources describing Alexander's life and deeds. Arrian, born in about AD 90, was a Greek who became a Roman citizen and official. His history of Alexander's campaigns, the *Anabasis Alexandri,* is thought to be the most reliable of the five sources. This is because Arrian based his work on two eyewitness histories that were later lost, both written by men who had known and worked under Alexander. Plutarch, a Greek born in the mid-first century AD, penned a large collection of biographies of Greek and Roman generals and statesmen. *Titled Parallel Lives,* it contains a fulsome, extremely colorful overview of Alexander based on a wide variety of ancient sources. The other three major sources for Alexander are the *Library of History,* by the first-century BC Sicilian Greek Diodorus Siculus; the *Epitome* of an obscure second-century AD Roman writer named Justin; and the *History of Quintus Curtius Rufus,* a first-century AD Roman historian. Though less authoritative than Arrian's and Plutarch's accounts, these three remain valuable because they include some information not mentioned in the other two.

accomplished, or revered. The ancients were strong believers in predestination, the idea that the gods sometimes bestowed special powers or fates on chosen humans. And these predictions and legends were the byproducts of such beliefs.

The reality of Alexander's conception and ancestry was considerably more mundane. When Alexander's father was born in about 382 BC, his homeland was a minor power and cultural backwater on the fringes of Greek civilization.

These maps show western Asia before Alexander's conquests.

At that time a majority of Greeks lived in hundreds of mostly small city-states spread across the Greek mainland and neighboring regions. These states saw themselves as separate nations. And they frequently fought one another to preserve their local territories and customs. Although the city-states featured a wide variety of governmental approaches, most were ruled by councils of citizens, often chosen by some sort of election.

In contrast, Macedonia, situated in the upper reaches of mainland Greece, was an ancient kingdom with a hereditary royal family. (Today, the word Macedonia refers to the ancient region as a kingdom or cultural sphere; the term Macedon is used to denote it as a political entity.) The Macedonians spoke Greek, and worshiped the same gods as other Greeks. However, most city-state Greeks had long looked upon their northern cousins as uncouth, uneducated, drunken ruffians. Major southern city-states such as Athens and Thebes were cultural and artistic centers as well as military powers. In particular, Athens was renowned for its poets, playwrights, sculptors, and painters. Because Macedonia lacked these refinements, it lay outside of Greece's cultural mainstream and was often the butt of jokes by other Greeks.

Macedonia's King Archelaus I, who reigned from 413 to 399 BC, tried his best to remedy this embarrassing situation. He set up a new capital at Pella, near the head of the Thermaic Gulf. This site had easier access to the gulf and the Aegean Sea beyond than the older capital of Aegae, lying to the southwest. (But the king retained Aegae as the burial site of Macedonia's kings.) Having made his royal court easier for other Greeks to reach, Archelaus invited many well-known Greek artists and intellectuals to live in Pella. Among them were the painter Zeuxis and playwright Euripides.

These earnest efforts were largely in vain, however. Archelaus was unable to solidly unite the Macedonian kingdom, which had long been divided into two distinct geographical regions. One, the so-called "lowlands," lay on a plain near the sea and included both Pella and Aegae. The "highlands" consisted of a rugged plateau rising farther inland. It was divided into a number of valleys and towns, each ruled by a tribal chief. These chiefs frequently resisted attempts by the lowland kings to create a unified, coherent Macedonian nation.

That daunting task was finally achieved by Alexander's father, Philip. Because he was the youngest of the three sons of King Amyntas III, Philip's chances of making it onto the throne initially seemed small. When Amyntas died in 368 BC, the eldest son became King Alexander II. The new monarch was soon assassinated, however, and the middle son, Perdiccas, became king. Finally, in 359 BC Perdiccas was killed in battle with the Illyrians, a tribal people who dwelled northwest of Macedonia. Technically, Perdiccas's son, Amyntas, was next in line for the kingship. But because he was still an infant, Philip was named his regent, or royal overseer. That meant that Philip, then twenty-two, held the real power, and less than two years later he took the throne. (Reasoning that Amyntas posed no credible threat, he allowed the boy to live.)

In the meantime, even while still regent, Philip wasted no time in exercising his newfound authority. Unlike his father and brothers, he was a natural leader with a cunning mind and a brilliant knack for both politics and military affairs. Immediately he saw that the key to bringing together the Macedonian lowlanders and highlanders was to establish a new national army.

Philip knew that the armies of the city-states were mostly militias.

King Philip *(Courtesy of Alinart/ Art Resources)*.

Alexander the Great *(Courtesy of Scala/Art Resources)*

UNLIKE HIS FATHER AND BROTHERS, HE WAS A NATURAL LEADER WITH A CUNNING MIND AND A BRILLIANT KNACK FOR BOTH POLITICS AND MILITARY AFFAIRS. IMMEDIATELY HE SAW THAT THE KEY TO BRINGING TOGETHER THE MACEDONIAN LOWLANDERS AND HIGHLANDERS WAS TO ESTABLISH A NEW NATIONAL ARMY.

A modern illustration depicts ancient Greek soldiers.

The soldiers, who were farmers and shopkeepers who fought only when called on by the government, were unpaid and had minimal training. (The main exception was Sparta, in southern Greece, where young men were trained as fearsome warriors from a young age.) By contrast, Philip rapidly created a permanent standing army, the first large, effective one in European history. He armed them appropriately and trained them rigorously. He also paid them a salary and promised them a portion of any spoils captured in wartime. According to the ancient Greek historian Diodorus Siculus, Philip "built up their morale, and, having improved the organization of his forces and equipped the men suitably with weapons of war, he held constant maneuvers of the men under arms and competitive drills. . . He was courteous [to the] men and sought to win over the multitudes by his gifts and his promises to the fullest loyalty, and endeavored to counteract by clever moves the crowd of impending dangers."

As a result of these wise moves, Philip induced large numbers of men from all over Macedonia to enlist, train, and fight together. Any highland chiefs who resisted his recruiting drives were in for a rude awakening. He either rounded up the chief's local supporters and shipped them to some remote region or took his children as hostages to ensure loyalty to and support for the crown. In these and other ways, Philip swiftly transformed the formerly fragmented kingdom into a strong nation under his direct control. Many years later, his son Alexander would summarize this remarkable achievement in a speech to his own soldiers:

> Philip found you a tribe of impoverished vagabonds, most of you dressed in skins, feeding a few sheep on the hills and fighting, feebly enough, to keep them from your neighbors. . . . He gave you cloaks to wear instead of skins; he brought you down from the hills into the plains; he taught you to fight on equal terms with the enemy on your borders, till you knew that your safety lay not, as once, in your mountain strongholds, but in your own valor. He made you city-dwellers; he brought you law; he civilized you.

Alexander was the product of one of the earliest of Philip's many marriages. A skilled diplomat, Philip regularly married the daughters of the rulers of opposing or neighboring states to help cement alliances with them. Alexander's mother, Olympias, was a princess of Epirus, a small kingdom west of Macedonia. As a child, the boy did not see his father very much because Philip was often away on military campaigns. So Olympias oversaw Alexander's early upbringing, and the two became extremely close.

A medallion bearing the effigy of Olympias, mother of Alexander *(Courtesy World History Archive/Alamy)*

Few substantial details have survived about Alexander's childhood. His exact physical characteristics are also somewhat uncertain. There is certainly no shortage of ancient depictions of him. According to Plutarch, "He was fair-skinned, with a ruddy tinge that showed itself especially upon his face and chest." A number of ancient portraits on coins, marble busts, and ivory carvings have also survived, as has the so-called Alexander Mosaic. Found in the ruins of an ancient Italian house, it shows the young Macedonian king in the midst of battle. These and other ancient renditions of Alexander depict him as an attractive youth with perfectly proportioned features. The problem is that most were made well after his death. They may well capture his general look; but by custom the artists tended to glamorize famous people by making them look more handsome and heroic than they really were.

Whatever Alexander looked like, as a young teenager he engaged in numerous activities arranged for him by his mother, nurses, and teachers. According to Plutarch, these included reading poetry, playing the flute and lyre (a small harp), acting in plays, hunting, and fighting with a wooden staff. Alexander was also an accomplished student. It was important to his parents, and to the Macedonian court in general, that he absorb as much traditional Greek culture as possible. Philip was concerned that other Greeks still viewed Macedonians as ill-bred country bumpkins. He wanted his family, courtiers, and especially his heir to appear well-educated and culturally refined. Alexander did not disappoint him. The young man read and came to admire the plays of the great fifth-century BC Athenian dramatists, as well as Homer's lengthy epic poems, the *Iliad* and *Odyssey.*

It was in the *Iliad,* of course, that Alexander first thrilled to the exploits of Achilles. Making the experience especially vivid was a copy of the epic that had been personally annotated by Greece's greatest living scholar, Aristotle. Moreover, that towering figure delivered the book in person. In Plutarch's words, Philip "considered that the task of training and educating his son was too important to be entrusted to the ordinary run of teachers . . . so he sent for Aristotle, the most famous and learned of the philosophers of his time."

Aristotle arrived in Pella in 343 BC and stayed for three years. He not only taught the royal prince about literature, political science, and ethics, but became a friend and mentor. The indelible mark that Aristotle left on his pupil can be seen in part by the manner in which Alexander treasured the copy of the *Iliad* he had been given. "He regarded the *Iliad* as a handbook of the art of war," Plutarch says, "and took [it] with him on his campaigns. . . .. He always kept [it] under his pillow together with his dagger."

Literature and other studies were not the only things that commanded young Alexander's attention. He seemed to be gripped by urgent longings for action and adult responsibilities, as if he did not have time to waste on childhood. In particular, he expressed the desire to go along with his father on military campaigns. At first, Philip said no. The young man would have plenty of time for fighting when he was older, the king said.

But this only frustrated Alexander and made him jealous of his father's political and battlefield exploits. "Whenever he heard that Philip had captured some famous city or won an overwhelming victory," Plutarch writes, "Alexander would show no pleasure at the news, but would declare to his friends, 'Boys, my father will forestall me in everything. There will be nothing great or spectacular for you and me to show the world.' He cared nothing for pleasure or wealth but only for deeds of valor and glory, and this was why he believed that the more he received from his father, the less would be left for him to conquer.'"

Eventually, however, Philip changed his mind. In 340 BC when Alexander was sixteen,

A 1895 painting of Greek philosopher Aristotle tutoring Alexander by American artist Jean Leon Gerome Ferris

PHILIP "CONSIDERED THAT THE TASK OF **TRAINING AND EDUCATING** HIS SON WAS TOO IMPORTANT TO BE ENTRUSTED TO THE ORDINARY RUN OF TEACHERS . . . SO HE SENT **FOR ARISTOTLE,** THE MOST FAMOUS **AND LEARNED** OF THE PHILOSOPHERS OF HIS TIME."

ALEXANDER TAMES BUCEPHALAS

Besides the derring-do of the heroes of the *Iliad*, another of young Alexander's passions was his love for a magnificent horse named Bucephalas, as recalled in Plutarch's account:

He was wild and quite unmanageable, for he would allow no one to mount him. . . . [Philip] became angry at being offered such a vicious animal [and] ordered it to be led away. But Alexander, who was standing close by. . . went quickly up to Bucephalas, took hold of his bridle, and turned him towards the sun. . . . He ran alongside the animal for a little way, calming him down by stroking him, and then [he] quietly threw aside his cloak and with a light spring vaulted safely onto his back. . . . When he saw that the horse was free of his fears, [he] urged him forward [and galloped away. Everyone present] broke into loud applause, while his father, we are told, actually wept for joy.

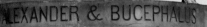

(Courtesy StockImages/ Alamy)

the king left on another campaign. And this time he gave his son the title of regent, leaving Alexander in complete charge of the government and royal court. No sooner had the king departed when Alexander swung into action, enacting a series of bold moves designed to prove his leadership abilities. Gathering some troops, he attacked a rebellious hill tribe and sacked their town. Then he deported the inhabitants, resettled the town with a mix of Macedonians and city-state Greeks, and renamed it Alexandropolis, after himself.

Such audacity was neither unheard-of nor original. Philip had earlier captured the Greek city of Crenides, resettled it, and renamed it Philippi. The difference was that Philip had done so as an established, powerful general. This time the feat had been accomplished by a sixteen-year-old with no military experience. The king could not help but be impressed, and one ancient account claims that "Philip became extravagantly fond of his son, so much so that he took pleasure in hearing the Macedonians speak of Alexander as their king and Philip as their general." The question was whether there was room in the kingdom, or in Greece for that matter, for two men of such formidable stature and ego. Time and circumstance would soon show that there was not.

The ruins of ancient Philippi, in northern Greece
(Courtesy Sean Burke/Alamy)

Bronze statue of Alexander astride Bucephalus, in Thessaloniki, capital of Greece's province of Macedonia. The statue was erected near Thessaloniki's waterfront in 1978. *(Courtesy StockImages/Alamy)*

CHAPTER TWO

IN PHILIP'S MIGHTY SHADOW

There is no doubt that Alexander grew up to be an inspiring leader and brilliant military general with a driving ambition to succeed. But it is likely that he would never have been able to achieve such tremendous success if not for his father. Whatever his inherent personal talents, Alexander was fortunate enough to be born a prince. From an early age he had as his role model a man who was extraordinarily talented and ambitious in his own right.

Furthermore, Philip created the conditions and tools that made it possible for his son to succeed and become more famous than himself. First, the older man unified his once-divided country and made it a world power. Then he organized and trained the finest army Europe had ever seen. Finally, and most importantly, Philip set in motion a series of conquests that created an expanding Macedonian empire.

After Philip's death, Alexander would inherit all of these unique and powerful tools and skillfully turn them to his own advantage. They were ready-made, so the young man would not have to invest decades in their creation, as Philip had. Also, they would make it possible for Alexander to indulge himself in feeding the urgent hunger for action and fame that seemed to haunt him always.

For the moment, however, Philip was very much alive. And no matter how great the prince's desire to prove himself a leader in his own right, like all other Macedonians he was still shrouded by the king's mighty shadow. When Alexander was still a toddler, that shadow began to creep outward past the kingdom's borders. It steadily threatened and then engulfed one neighboring state after another. Meanwhile, as the boy grew he watched and learned from his father. Philip consistently used an effective combination of diplomacy, practical politics, and sheer force to impose his will on Greece. Even if he was reluctant to admit it, Alexander was both impressed by and jealous of these achievements. And he would later use this same mixture of tactics to impose his own will and goals on others.

Making possible the "sheer force" component of this potent mixture was the national army that in many ways had put Macedonia on the historical map. As a teenager Alexander witnessed this formidable force in action. Moreover, he actually fought in it under his father's command and later took charge of it himself. A closer examination of Philip's army reveals some of the keys to both his and his son's remarkable series of successes.

Philip's military reforms were characterized by the innovative and highly effective use of existing soldiers, battlefield units, and weapons. Nearly all armies before his, Greek and non-Greek, had employed both infantry (foot soldiers) and cavalry (mounted fighters). But in Greece, infantrymen had traditionally formed the core units and done most of the primary fighting. This was partly because breeding strong horses and training cavalrymen were both costly.

More crucially, stirrups had not yet been invented. This made it difficult for a horseman to stay on his mount, particularly if he was weighted down by heavy armor. Therefore, horse soldiers were usually light-armed, and direct cavalry charges on infantry, called shock action, were almost never attempted for fear of unseating most of the attackers. Cavalry was instead used to throw javelins from a distance, to guard the flanks and rear of infantry units, and to chase down fleeing enemies.

Philip turned this approach on its head. He made up for the lack of stirrups by having his horsemen train and practice much longer. Better at staying mounted during battle, these riders became adept at shock action. Philip armed them with a long cavalry lance, the *xyston,* and had them make frontal attacks on lightly armed infantry. These elite riders were recruited from the

Fighting hoplites depicted on a piece of ancient Greek pottery
(ca 560 BC-550 BC), at the Louvre in Paris.

ranks of the nobility. An earlier Macedonian king, Alexander I, had organized a group of young aristocrats to guard his person. They were known as the *hetairoi*, or "King's Companions." Philip made them the core of his offensive cavalry force, which appropriately came to be called the Companion Cavalry. Near the end of his reign, he had more than 2,000 of these elite horsemen.

Philip was equally innovative with his infantry. Before his time, Greek heavy infantrymen, known as hoplites, fought in a battlefield formation called a phalanx. It consisted of a long, rectangular block of men standing in ranks, or lines, one arrayed behind another. On average there were eight ranks. But some generals called for more or fewer ranks. The soldiers wielded thrusting spears about six or seven feet long, which they jabbed at their opponents. (Each also carried a sword, but this was usually a backup weapon a fighter resorted to only if his spear broke.)

The traditional Greek phalanx was an extremely formidable offensive force. But Philip made it even more effective and lethal. He doubled its depth to sixteen ranks, and dispensed with the thrusting spear. Instead, he armed his infantrymen, the *pezhetairoi*, or "Foot Companions," with two-handed pikes called *sarissas*. These were probably about twelve to fifteen feet long at first. Later they reached eighteen feet or more.

An engraving shows the Macedonian phalanx
in action during the Battle of the Carts.

The men in the first few ranks of the unit, which became known as the Macedonian phalanx, lowered their pikes as they approached an enemy. The pike-points projected outward from the front row, creating a deadly barrier of wood and metal that no attacker could penetrate. Philip's cavalry and infantry improvements, combined with a mastery he gained in siege tactics, made him a force to reckon with in mainland Greece and surrounding regions.

Philip's military reforms constituted only part of the formidable legacy he passed on to Alexander. The father also imparted to the son a thirst for conquest and domination of foreign lands. At some point Philip decided to expand his and his kingdom's power and influence over neighboring states. Over time that goal grew in scope. And eventually he sought to conquer all of mainland Greece and become leader of a confederation, or alliance, of Greek states.

That such a lofty goal was even feasible was due in part to the fact that the city-states, including Athens, Sparta, Corinth, and Thebes, were disunited and war-weary. A half century before, the twenty-seven-year-long

THE MACEDONIAN PHALANX

In his *Histories,* the second-century BC Greek historian Polybius describes the Macedonian phalanx, a version of which still existed in his time:

There are a number of factors which make it easy to understand that so long as the phalanx retains its characteristic form and strength, nothing can withstand its charge or resist it face to face. When the phalanx is closed up for action, each man. . . occupies a space of three feet. . . . The pike he carries . . . will protect fifteen feet in front of [him] when he advances against the enemy

Statue of Polybius outside the Austrian Parliament building in Vienna
(Courtesy Clive Sawyer/Alamy)

grasping it with both hands. . . . It follows that each man in the front rank will have the points of five pikes extending in front of him, each point being three feet ahead of the one behind. From these facts we can easily picture the nature and the tremendous power of a charge by the whole phalanx, when it advances sixteen deep with leveled pikes. . . . Those who are stationed further back than the fifth [rank hold their pikes] with the points tilted upwards over the shoulders of the men in front. In this way they give protection to the whole phalanx from above, for the pikes are massed so closely that they can keep off any [arrows or javelins] which might clear the heads of the front ranks.

The modern-day town of Kalambaka in Thessaly, one of the Greek regions overrun by Philip. *(Courtesy Kuttig-Travel/Alamy)*

Peloponnesian War had pit Greek against Greek. The conflict had engulfed and exhausted most Greek states. And that had left them vulnerable to attack by an outside power.

Philip expertly exploited this weakness. In the process, he taught his son the most effective ways of threatening, intimidating, surprising, and outfighting opponents. At first Alexander was too young to actually take part in foreign affairs. So he had to be content with hearing about his father's conquests secondhand. Also, while campaigning, Philip sent letters to the young man, some of which offered practical advice on how to divide and manipulate one's adversaries. According to Plutarch, the king counseled Alexander to make friends with both "good and bad" men in the cities he ruled. Later, Philip said, he could make use of the good ones by collecting favors from them; he could also suppress the bad ones at his leisure by killing or exiling them. Meanwhile, said Philip, the prince should go out of his way to "behave himself courteously toward the Macedonians, and to acquire influence with the people."

When Alexander was ten, in 346 BC, his father marched part of his army into southern Greece. Philip had already captured several key cities

A medallion of Philip II of Macedon
(Courtesy World History Archive/Alamy)

PHILIP EXPERTLY **EXPLOITED** THIS WEAKNESS. IN THE PROCESS, HE TAUGHT HIS SON THE MOST EFFECTIVE WAYS OF **THREATENING, INTIMIDATING,** SURPRISING, AND OUTFIGHTING OPPONENTS.

lying on or near the northern Aegean coast. He had also made himself master of Thessaly, the large agricultural and horse-breeding state occupying the central part of the Greek mainland.

During these early conquests, the popular Athenian orator Demosthenes had repeatedly sounded warnings. "He cannot rest content with what he has conquered," Demosthenes said of Philip. "He is always taking in more, everywhere casting his net around us, while we sit idle and do nothing. When, Athenians, will you take the necessary action?" But few Athenians and other Greeks heeded these words. Most had viewed Philip as a mere pirate or thug who would not dare to move directly on the powerful southern city-states.

Now that Philip had made that fateful move, the southern Greeks expressed shock. "The news stunned the Athenians," Plutarch reports. "Nobody knew what advice should be given, [and Athenian leaders were] struck dumb and appeared to be completely at a loss." As before, only Demosthenes seemed able to voice the necessary words of outrage and caution. "If anyone imagines that all this imports no danger to our city," he said, "I must express my astonishment, and beg you all alike to. . . regard Philip as our enemy. . . . All his intrigues are directed against Athens. [Be warned that] he wants to rule, and he has made up his mind that you, and only you, are his rivals. . . . He is wide awake and ready to strike."

Philip took his time, however. Having intruded into the south, he carefully consolidated his position before attempting any more expansion. This was another lesson that Alexander took to heart. Later, during his own conquests, he would time and again make sure to secure and strengthen his recent gains before pressing onward.

Thus, it was not until 338 BC that Philip felt ready to confront the major city-states. By this time, Alexander had already defeated the group of rebels and established a new city while serving as royal regent. Evidently Philip felt that these feats were enough proof that the young man was ready to stand with his father on the battlefield. Looking forward to his first test as a commander, Alexander, then eighteen, joined Philip in south-central Greece. Together they led the Macedonian army eastward into Theban territory.

In the Cephisus Valley, near Chaeronea, a town not far west of Thebes, Philip and Alexander found their path blocked by a large army. The Athenians and Thebans had finally listened to Demosthenes' rants about

A drawing of Demosthenes before the Athenian Council by Louis Loeb, 1898 *(Courtesy StockImages/Alamy)*

Map of ancient Greece and its cities *(Courtesy StockImages/Alamy)*

Philip. Hoping to halt the Macedonian advance, they hastily organized a coalition of local Greek forces. The allied army's right wing was made up of some 12,000 Theban hoplites led by the famous Sacred Band. Its three hundred members were handpicked, elite fighters who were at least a match for the best of Philip's own warriors. On the allied left stood 10,000 Athenians, Demosthenes himself in their ranks. And in the middle were arrayed smaller contingents from other southern city-states.

On August 4, 338 BC, Philip made the decision to attack. Of his 30,000 infantry, an unknown number were pikemen in the mighty Macedonian phalanx. This unit he placed in his center. He himself led another large unit of foot soldiers on the right wing, opposite the Athenians in the allied left wing. Meanwhile, Alexander commanded the Companion Cavalry, 2,000 strong, in the Macedonian left wing. This was an unprecedented honor and weighty responsibility for someone so young.

At first, the Macedonian right and middle units moved slowly forward toward the waiting enemy. But then they stopped and began backing up, as if the men had been seized by fear and indecision. Of course, it was only a trick devised by the wily Philip.

It worked.

As he had hoped, the Athenians took the bait and lurched forward at the run, some of them shouting "Come on, let's drive them back to Macedonia!" As the charge continued, the Athenians steadily moved away from the other allies. Per Philip's plan, this created a gap in the allied line, into which Alexander rushed at the head of his well-armed cavalrymen. According to Diodorus: "Alexander, his heart set on showing his father his prowess . . . succeeded in. . . striking down many [men as] he bore heavily on the [allied] troops opposite him. [Dead bodies] piled up until finally Alexander forced his way through the line and put his opponents to flight."

While this was happening, Philip suddenly ordered his infantrymen to reverse their backpedaling and plunge forward. Caught by surprise, some of the onrushing Athenians met grisly deaths, run through by the giant mass of sharpened pikes protruding from the front of the Macedonian phalanx. The rest turned tail and ran for their lives. Of the entire allied line, only the stalwart troops of the Theban Sacred Band stood their ground. They were soon surrounded by Philip's pikemen and Alexander's horsemen. Against impossible odds, these courageous individuals chose to fight to the death. The forty-six of their number whom the Macedonians managed to capture alive were dragged away still resisting with all their might.

Philip was duly impressed by these fearless fighters. But he sensed that he would not have to face their like again. His sweeping victory at Chaeronea had broken the main resistance to his conquest of Greece. And any negotiations by the losers would proceed on his terms. As for Alexander, he had shown himself to be an effective commander worthy of eventually filling his father's shoes. What he could not then foresee was that those shoes would need to be filled far sooner than expected.

THE SACRED BAND

Plutarch penned the following description of the Theban Sacred Band, whose members made a heroic last stand on the bloody field of Chaeronea:

[The unit] consisted of three hundred picked men, who were given their training and lodging by the city. . . . This force was composed of lovers and beloved. . . . A band which is united by the ties of love is truly indissoluble and unbreakable, since both lovers and beloved are ashamed to be disgraced in the presence of the other, and each stands his ground at a moment of danger to protect the other. . . .. [The Sacred Band] was never defeated until the battle of Chaeronea. [When] King Philip. . . was inspecting the dead after the fighting, he stood at the place where the three hundred had faced the long pikes of his phalanx, and lay dead in their armor, their bodies piled one upon the other. He was amazed at the sight, and when he learned that this was the band of lovers. . . he wept and exclaimed, "A curse on those who imagine that these men ever did or suffered anything shameful."

Macedonian forces led by Philip and Alexander defeat the Thebans and
Athenians at Chaeronea in 338 BC.
(Courtesy Mary Evans Picture Library/Alamy)

Macedonia's Alexander III, later called "the Great"
(Courtesy The Print Collector/Alamy)

CHAPTER THREE

A NEW
MACEDONIAN
KING

The defeat of the major city-states at Chaeronea was an important turning point not only in Greek history but also in Alexander's life. Despite his tender age, he had led the Macedonian cavalry in the victory and killed many men. He was no longer a child, and now faced the rigorous political responsibilities that went with being the kingdom's prince and royal heir.

To Alexander's regret, some of these duties could be routine and boring. In the wake of the great battle, for instance, Philip sent his son to Illyria. There the young man paid official visits to some local rulers who owed allegiance to Macedonia because Philip had defeated their small kingdoms.

Such mundane obligations turned out to be short-lived, however. Less than a year after his Illyrian trip, Alexander would find himself thrust into a whirlwind of political turmoil and change. When Philip was assassinated in 336 BC, Alexander had to replace his father on Macedonia's throne. At the time this was a position of enormous and difficult responsibility because much more than the Macedonian kingdom was involved. Having defeated the leading city-states, Philip had made himself their overseer. And Alexander now had to assume that weighty and challenging office. Whether he would succeed or fail as king would turn on how he exercised control over and exploited the resources of the conquered Greek states.

Meanwhile, Alexander could not escape the emotional effects of acquiring such huge power and responsibility at such a young age. For years he had felt a sense of special destiny and an urgency to fulfill it quickly. And those feelings appear to have been heightened by his elevation to the highest office in Greece at the age of twenty.

As for how to maintain order in Greece, Alexander could once more turn to the example his father had set. In the short period between his victory at Chaeronea and his untimely death, Philip had displayed a political adeptness and managerial talent that matched his battlefield brilliance. In the wake of the battle, he had wisely treated each former enemy differently, depending on the threat it posed and its potential usefulness. Thebes had been the chief military power among the city-states. So he dealt with the Thebans fairly harshly. He killed or took the estates of a number of Theban leaders and ordered a large contingent of Macedonian troops to occupy Thebes on a permanent basis.

In contrast, Alexander noted, Philip dealt far more leniently with the Athenians. No Athenian leaders were executed, not even Philip's outspoken critic Demosthenes. Nor were any Macedonian troops sent to patrol Athens. In addition, Philip allowed the 2,000 Athenians he had captured at Chaeronea to return home. The reasons for this generous treatment of Athens were twofold. First, Athens was Greece's chief cultural center, and Philip wanted to gain a reputation as a supporter of Greek culture. Second, Athens possessed the largest navy in Greece—more than three hundred warships. Philip reasoned that these vessels would come in handy in future conquests he was already thinking about.

Philip made it clear that other city-states would be treated as well as Athens so long as they went along with his grandiose plans for Greece. These plans had two main goals. The first was to unify the Greek-speaking states into a large-scale confederation headed by Macedonia. Philip required each city-state to send representatives to a *synedrion,* or great meeting, which he oversaw. It became known as the Congress of Corinth, after the city in southern Greece where it was held.

At the meeting, the Greeks agreed to form the alliance Philip desired. Called the League of Corinth, it was ruled by a council made up of delegates from the various states. The council established a perpetual alliance with Macedonia. And Philip acted as *hegemon,* or leader, of the league's joint military forces, with the title of Captain-General. Although Philip did not officially name himself ruler of all Greece, in an unofficial sense he was just that. One of the league's rules said that member states had to obey without question any orders given by the *hegemon.* So it was clear to all that Philip held the real power and could impose his will in any manner he chose. Another rule said that if Philip died his successor would inherit his lofty position and powers. That meant that Alexander was squarely in line to become supreme master of the Greeks.

OATH OF THE LEAGUE MEMBERS

Philip insisted that all members of the League of Corinth swear an oath to him. It remained the same under Alexander, with the exception of substituting his name for his father's.

I SWEAR BY ZEUS, EARTH, SUN, POSEIDON, ATHENA, ARES, AND ALL THE GODS AND GODDESSES. I WILL ABIDE BY THE PEACE; I WILL NOT BREAK THE AGREEMENTS WITH PHILIP THE MACEDONIAN; NOR WILL I TAKE UP ARMS WITH HOSTILE INTENT AGAINST ANY ONE OF THOSE WHO ABIDE BY THE OATHS EITHER BY LAND OR BY SEA.

The other major goal Philip had for Greece, which Alexander inherited along with the league, was to mount a major military campaign against the Persian Empire. Centered in what are now Iraq and Iran, it was the largest empire the world had seen up to that time. In the previous century, an enormous Persian army led by King Xerxes had attacked Greece. Rising to the challenge, the tiny Greek states had managed to defeat the invaders and drive them away. But in the years that followed, Persia remained a perpetual nemesis, frequently scheming to promote division among the Greeks.

As time went on, Greek orators occasionally called for Greece to get revenge against its old foe by invading the Persian Empire. But none of these pleas were seriously considered until the Athenian orator Isocrates addressed some open letters to Philip. Isocrates declared, "Perhaps there are those... who will venture to rebuke [scold] me because I have chosen to challenge you to the task of leading the expedition against the barbarians [i.e., the Persians]. . . . What a disgrace it is to sit idly by and see Asia flourishing more than Europe and the barbarians enjoying a greater prosperity than the Hellenes (Greeks). . . . We must not allow this state of affairs to go on; no, we must change and reverse it entirely."

Philip announced his plans to move against Persia at a League of Corinth meeting in 337 BC. Avenging the past Persian invasion of Greece was only a convenient excuse, of course. Philip's real motive was to extend Macedonian power over as much of the known world as he could. As a preliminary move, he sent his trusted generals Parmenio and Attalus to secure the area around the Hellespont (now the Dardanelles, the narrow strait separating Greece from Asia Minor). Across that waterway he planned to lead a united Macedonian and Greek army into Asia.

It was Alexander, and not Philip, however, who was destined to lead that momentous campaign because the king was suddenly assassinated in 336 BC. Along with numerous other members of the Macedonian court, the twenty-year-old prince witnessed the event himself. Some historians speculate that Alexander himself was involved in the murder plot, although if so he was careful to erase any evidence of his role. The royal father and son had not been getting along very well in the year prior to the assassination. In 337, Philip had taken a new wife—Cleopatra, a young woman related to the general Attalus. Olympias felt snubbed and, taking his mother's side, Alexander publicly ridiculed his father during the wedding celebration. As

Plutarch tells it:

> Attalus, who had drunk too much at the banquet, called upon the Macedonians to pray to the gods that the union of Philip and Cleopatra might bring forth a legitimate heir to the throne. Alexander flew into a rage at these words, shouted at him, "Villain, do you take me for a bastard, then?" and hurled a drinking-cup at his head. At this Philip lurched to his feet, and drew his sword against his son, but fortunately for them both he was so overcome with drink and with rage that he tripped and fell headlong. Alexander jeered at him and cried out, "Here is the man who was making ready to cross from Europe to Asia, and who cannot even cross from one table to another without losing his balance."

Alexander's possible involvement in the murder aside, the actual deed was committed by a young Macedonian nobleman named Pausanias. After stabbing the king, Pausanias fled. But before he could get very far several of Alexander's friends caught up and killed him with their spears.

SOME HISTORIANS SPECULATE THAT **ALEXANDER HIMSELF WAS INVOLVED IN THE MURDER PLOT,** ALTHOUGH IF SO HE WAS CAREFUL TO ERASE ANY EVIDENCE OF HIS ROLE. THE ROYAL FATHER AND SON HAD NOT BEEN GETTING ALONG VERY WELL IN THE YEAR PRIOR TO **THE ASSASSINATION.**

DEATH IN A THEATER

According to Diodorus, the assassination occurred in a theater in which the king, Alexander, and others were taking part in a wedding party for Philip's daughter:

Philip appeared wearing a white cloak, and by his express orders his bodyguard held away from him and followed only at a distance, since he wanted to show publicly that he was protected by the goodwill of all the Greeks and had no need of a guard. . . . When [Pausanias] saw that the king was left alone, [he] rushed at him, pierced him [with a dagger] through his ribs, and stretched him out dead; then [he] ran for the... horses which he had prepared for his flight.

A hand-colored woodcut of a nineteenth-century illustration
of the assassination of King Philip.
(Courtesy of North Wind Picture Archives/Alamy)

Per Macedonian custom, while Philip's body was still warm Alexander summoned all the military officers and soldiers in the area. Standing before them in the blood-soaked theater, he presented himself as the former king's rightful heir and asked for their approval. And they gave it, beating their spears against their shields and shouting Alexander's name over and over. He was now officially Alexander III, ruler of Macedonia.

Alexander realized that getting the support of his fellow Macedonians was one thing, but the allegiance of other Greeks was quite another. When news of Philip's death spread, people in most city-states were jubilant. And many in Thebes and Athens celebrated and called for breaking the alliance they had recently made with Macedonia. To make it clear that the new Macedonian king was no less formidable than the old one, Alexander immediately marched southward at the head of a small army.

Reaching Thessaly, he reaffirmed that state's loyalty. Then he pushed on to Thebes and Athens, where people were astounded by his dis-

Alexander became king after the assassination of his father, as depicted in this hand-colored nineteenth-century illustration.
(*Courtesy North Wind Picture Archives*)

play of speed and resolve. Leaders in those states quickly apologized for their recent behavior. Alexander accepted their apologies. Finally, he met with the League council to make sure its members harbored no doubts that as Greece's captain-general, he would tolerate no disloyalty. In these ways, without striking a single blow, the brash new Macedonian king effectively solidified the huge power base Philip had left him.

Satisfied that he had pacified southern Greece, Alexander wasted no time in returning home. Word had come that several tribes in Thrace, the region lying north of the Aegean Sea, had rebelled against Macedonia. It was vital to put down the insurrections. The narrow waterways that passed through the area connected the Aegean and Black seas, and rebel control of these channels threatened to disrupt a major portion of Greece's commerce.

Feeling his usual sense of urgency, Alexander opted to deal with the problem at once. Leaving Philip's capable general Antipater in charge in Pella, the young king hurried into Thrace. At Mt. Haemus, on the far side of the Nestus River, he encountered a large force of rebels. "They had collected a number of carts," Arrian later wrote, which they planned to send

> crashing down on the Macedonian phalanx as the men were climbing the steepest part of the slope. Their hope was that the impact of the vehicles would cause damage to the enemy troops . . . . [Alexander's] orders were that those sections of the heavy infantry which had room enough were to break formation when the carts came tearing down the slope, and so let them through. [Those men directly in the carts' path were to lie] prone on the ground with shields locked together above heir bodies, so as to give the heavy wagons. . . a chance to bounce over the top of them without doing any harm.

Alexander quickly quelled the revolts in Thrace, then was forced to move westward to deal with similar uprisings in Illyria. In a series of lightning campaigns, he easily defeated the rebels. However, before he made it back to Macedonia, someone spread the false rumor that he had been killed in battle. As before, many Greeks celebrated what they thought was an end to Macedonia's iron grip on them. In Thebes, emboldened citizens laid siege to the Cadmea, the city's fortified central hill. There, the Macedonian soldiers who had been occupying Thebes held out as best as they could, hoping that Alexander would rescue them.

That hope was not in vain. Having led an army southward in a swift forced march, the king appeared before the city, taking the Thebans by surprise. To their credit, they continued to resist. But they had no chance against the well-trained Macedonian troops, whom Alexander let loose to destroy the city. Nearly every building was leveled. The only exceptions were the temples and the house of the renowned Theban poet Pindar. From his father, Alexander had learned the importance of sparing an enemy's religious and cultural icons to help avert the familiar charges of Macedonian barbarism. "As for the population of Thebes," Plutarch says, Alexander "singled out the priests, a few citizens who had friendly connections with Macedonia, the descendants of the poet Pindar, and those who had opposed the revolt to be spared. All the rest were publicly sold into slavery to the number of twenty thousand. Those who were killed in the battle numbered more than six thousand."

A handful of Thebans who openly resisted Alexander did manage to escape his wrath. They were a widow named Timocleia and her children. When Macedonian soldiers broke into her home, one raped her and then demanded to know where she kept her gold. She led him to her deep garden well and said that she had thrown her valuables into it a few hours before. Falling for the ruse, the man leaned over, hoping to catch sight of the loot. The woman promptly pushed him down the shaft and dropped heavy stones onto him until he was dead. Other soldiers tied Timocleia up and brought her to Alexander, who asked who she was. "I am the sister of Theagenes," she replied in a defiant tone, "who commanded our army against your father, Philip, and fell at Chaeronea fighting for the liberty of Greece." So impressed was Alexander with her display of courage in the face of certain death that he let her and her family go.

Alexander next considered what to do about Athens. Its people had not openly rebelled, as the Thebans had. But several leading Athenians, including Demosthenes, had called for such action when they thought Alexander was dead. At first, Alexander demanded that the city hand these troublemakers over to him. But then he received a visit from the Athenian statesman Phocion, a distinguished individual known for his honesty, diplomacy, and courage who had been admired and trusted by Philip. When the two met, the king put aside his anger and listened to the older man's petition and advice. Phocion urged Alexander to show mercy to his fellow Athenians, despite their rash behavior. The visitor advised the king, according to Plutarch, that "If it was peace that Alexander wanted above all, then he should make an end of the fighting, but if it was glory, then he should transfer the theater of war and turn his arms away from Greece against the [Persians]. Phocion spoke at length and his words were well chosen to fit Alexander's character and aspirations, with the result that he quite transformed the king's mood and allayed his resentment against the Athenians."

Impatient as always, and urged on by Phocion, Alexander stepped up the preparations for a campaign against the Persians. Only eight months after sacking Thebes, he set out for the Hellespont at the head of a large army. The histories and fates of the Greeks and many other peoples were about to be altered in ways that no one, including Alexander, could begin to imagine.

An eighteenth-century engraving of Greek poet Pindar
(Courtesy Interfoto/Alamy)

A colored rendering of a modern woodcut shows Alexander charging
into battle atop his faithful Bucephalas.

CHAPTER FOUR

ASSAULT ON THE
GREATEST
EMPIRE

n the spring of 334 BC, Alexander began his daring, historic assault
on Persia, the greatest empire the world had yet known. Sometime in
May he and his troops reached Sestus, near the shore of the Hellespont.
There, the young king ceremoniously set up twelve altars, each dedicated to
one of the traditional Olympian gods that the Greeks revered. The leader of
these deities was the mighty Zeus, who was also the divine protector of safe
landings. It seemed appropriate to offer sacrifices to Zeus and the other gods
to ensure the army's safe landing in Asia.

When these religious duties concluded, the soldiers climbed onto
boats and made the crossing. The exact spot they embarked from is unknown. But it is likely that they chose a place where the channel was nar-
rowest—about a mile. Ancient historian Diodorus claimed that as his vessel
approached the opposite shore, Alexander threw a spear onto the beach.
Then, he leaped out of the boat, "signifying that received Asia from the gods
as a spear-won prize."

Having landed in Asia Minor, Persian territory, Alexander first visited the ruins of Troy, which were situated near the Hellespont. This must
have been truly thrilling for him because he viewed it as a revered spot
and had read so much about the Trojan War in the *Iliad*. It was the place

A modern statue depicts Athena, goddess of wisdom and war.

where his hero Achilles had fought and died!

There were also personal and religious dimensions to the visit. Alexander claimed to be descended from another hero of the Trojan War—Neoptolemus—and believed that the same gods who had given the Greeks victory at Troy centuries before would now grant him a victory over Persia. To this end, he made prayers and sacrifices to Troy's patron goddess, Athena (the Greek deity of war and wisdom).

Whatever divine aid Alexander thought he could count on, his main confidence in attaining victory lay in the quality of his army. At its core were the well-trained Macedonian forces that Philip had created and passed on to his heir. Alexander had also taken along a number of cavalrymen, archers, and other fighters from various Greek states. Together, the assembled soldiers formed an allied Greek army of tremendous diversity, with numerous individual skills, fighting styles, and strengths.

The centerpiece of these forces was the Macedonian phalanx. In the early months of Alexander's campaigns it consisted of about 9,000 infantrymen divided into six battalions (or brigades) called *taxeis*. For organizational purposes, each taxis broke down further into three *lochoi*, or companies, of about five hundred men each. On the battlefield, each *lochos* formed a block-like portion of the phalanx measuring thirty-two men wide and sixteen men deep. The beauty of this system was that all 9,000 men could operate in unison, becoming a giant, indomitable fighting unit, or if Alexander so chose, the battalions could operate individually or in groups, creating in effect two or more smaller phalanxes.

Another key Macedonian infantry unit was made up of fighters called the Hypaspists. About 3,000 strong, they were heavily armed like the members of the phalanx. But the Hypaspists were more of an elite or specialty unit that both Philip and Alexander used in a variety of ways depending on the situation. These soldiers sometimes acted as the king's personal bodyguard. On other occasions they guarded one or both flanks of the phalanx, which were otherwise vulnerable to enemy attack. Another possible role for the Hypaspists was to go on the offense along with the phalanx.

Alexander also had a number of light-armed infantry units from across mainland Greece and the Aegean islands. Among them were about five-hundred archers from Crete and several thousand Greek hoplites armed with the traditional thrusting spear.

As for his cavalry, Alexander entered Asia Minor with about 5,000 horsemen. Approximately 1,800 to 2,000 of them were the elite Companions, who broke down into several squadrons called *ilai*. A typical *ile* consisted of about two hundred men. Alexander's other cavalry units came from various Greek kingdoms, regions, and city-states, including Paeonia, Thrace, and Thessaly.

Artist Johnny Shumate's reconstruction of a Macedonian Hypaspist

ALEXANDER'S ARMY ON THE MARCH

One of the chief strengths of Alexander's army was its efficient organization off as well as on the battlefield. When on the march, the army broke down into small, platoon-sized units whose members traveled and rested together. The basic marching unit of the phalanx, for example, was the dekas, consisting of one file (straight line) of sixteen men. A dekas was commanded by a sergeant-like officer called a dekadarch. Each dekas was assigned its own servant to oversee the tents and other heavy baggage. The number of tents used by a single dekas is unknown. More certain is that each man in the unit carried his own pack, which contained a bedroll, drinking cup, food, and a few personal items. For comfort, when traveling a man carried his helmet and donned a beret-like cap known as a kausia.

Although Alexander's army was diverse, well-armed, and highly versatile, to achieve success it needed a talented commanding general. And in Alexander, it had one of the finest military strategists of the ancient world. He often displayed an innate grasp of what an enemy planned to do and was able to formulate an effective counter-plan on a moment's notice. He also inspired his men by fighting alongside them in battle, usually at the head of the Companion horsemen.

In addition, Alexander had a keen grasp of logistics, the management of the flow of supplies. His agents maintained an extremely effective network of supply depots that made sure the army had the estimated 135 tons of grain and 70,000 gallons of water it required each day. Finally, Alexander was careful to watch his back. Despite his tendency to act impulsively, as if he had no time to waste, beforehand he almost always made sure the territory behind him was secure. That way he could not be trapped or surrounded by an enemy.

Alexander demonstrated his defensive tactics almost immediately after crossing into Asia Minor. His initial goal was to march down the eastern Aegean coast. The numerous Greek cities of that region, then called Ionia, had been under Persian domination for some time, and he planned to liberate them. Before he had gone far, however, his scouts announced that a large enemy army was approaching from the east. He could have bypassed it

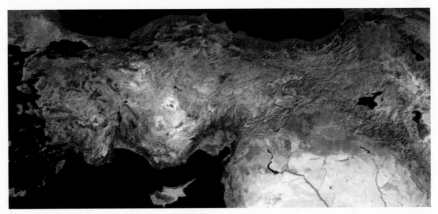

Composite satellite image of Asia Minor (now Turkey)

ALEXANDER HAD A KEEN **GRASP OF LOGISTICS,** THE MANAGEMENT OF THE FLOW OF SUPPLIES. HIS AGENTS MAINTAINED AN EXTREMELY EFFECTIVE NETWORK OF SUPPLY DEPOTS THAT MADE SURE THE ARMY HAD THE ESTIMATED **135 TONS OF GRAIN & 70,000 GALLONS OF WATER** IT REQUIRED EACH DAY.

and continued south. But that would have allowed Persian forces to surround him and cut off his supply channels. So he collected his Macedonians and a few Greek allies and hurried to intercept the enemy.

The opposing army was stationed on the eastern bank of the Granicus River, about forty miles east of the Hellespont. It consisted of about 20,000 cavalry commanded by the satraps (governors) of the local Persian provinces. These men, among them Arsites, Arsames, and Spithridates, reported directly to the Persian king, Darius III. But they exercised considerable autonomy and were responsible for raising their own troops. The Persian commanders also had infantry: 5,000 Greek mercenary hoplites led by Memnon, a native of the Greek Aegean island of Rhodes.

When Alexander's army reached the river, his second in command, Parmenio, a trusted general who had served under Philip, urged caution. It would be best to wait until the next day, he said. That would allow enough time to fully assess the situation and draw up a sound battle plan. But Alexander, driven by his usual sense of urgency, refused to wait. He placed his phalanx and Hypaspists in the center, while he took charge of the cavalry on the right wing and put Parmenio at the head of the left-wing horsemen.

At first, as Arrian recalls, "There was a profound hush as both armies stood for a while motionless on the brink of the river, as if in awe of what was to come." Then Alexander signaled his trumpeters to sound the charge and led his Companions into the river. As the horsemen fought against the strong current, the Persians showered them with volleys of arrows. Finally, the Macedonian cavalry reached the opposite bank. And there, Arrian continues, "a hand-to-hand struggle developed, the Macedonian mounted troops trying to force their way out of the water, the Persians doing their utmost to prevent them. . . . It was a cavalry battle with, as it were, infantry tactics: horse against horse, man against man, locked together."

As the fighting progressed, the Persian commanders sent troops from their center to deal with Alexander's assault on their left wing. As he had anticipated, this weakened the Persian center, making it easier for the phalanx to cross the river and attack. As it did so, Alexander penetrated the enemy ranks until he came face to face with some of the Persian satraps and nobles. Lunging forward, he jammed his lance into the face of one of them; seconds later, he stabbed another through the chest. The stroke was so forceful that he either broke his lance or could not remove it from the dead man's body.

An engraving by French artist Jean Andre Castaigne of the fierce struggle
of Alexander's calvary, led by himself, at the ford of the river in the battle
of the Granicus. Castaigne created more than thirty-six art pieces about
Alexander the Great for an 1898-1899 series. An illustrator and engraver,
Castaigne worked for *Harper's*, the *Century*, a popular quarterly, and
Scribners, providing more than 160 illustrations.

Seeing his enemy's predicament, Spithridates rode up and raised his sword to strike. Fortunately for Alexander, his officer and friend Cleitus sliced off the satrap's sword arm in a single blow, saving the young king's life.

As the savage fighting continued, the Persian troops realized that most of their commanders had been slain. They also saw that they were being surrounded by Alexander's cavalry and infantry units. So the bulk of the Persian cavalry suddenly turned and fled.

Instead of giving chase, as was his usual custom, Alexander turned to deal with Memnon's mercenaries, who had yet to enter the fray. These hoplites had backed up to a patch of high ground overlooking the river. They were skilled, tough veterans who could easily have bested almost any enemy infantry in the world. But their six-foot spears were no match for the bristling array of pikes in the onrushing phalanx. "Alexander quickly had them surrounded," Arrian writes, "and butchered." Around 3,000 of the mercenaries were slaughtered where they stood, while the other 2,000 surrendered and were led away in chains. Memnon was not among them, as he had managed to escape.

The first major battle of Alexander's Asian conquests had been an overwhelming victory. In addition to the 3,000 mercenaries killed, the Persians lost between 1,000 and 2,000 horsemen. In comparison, the Macedonian and allied losses totaled only about eighty-five cavalry and thirty infantry.

Such lopsided casualty figures had been and would continue to be a hallmark of Alexander's military campaigns. They stemmed not only from his superb army and personal talents as a commander, but also from his affinity for brutality and mass destruction unmatched by most military leaders, both ancient and modern. The merciless destruction of Thebes and the unnecessary massacre of Memnon's Greeks (who might have been persuaded to join Alexander) were only two of many examples.

To Alexander, it wasn't enough to simply best his enemies in battle. He felt that for true victory to be achieved, he had to fully annihilate his enemies, and their very culture and way of life that led them to oppose him at all. As such, Alexander often insisted on wiping his enemies out, leading to massive numbers of casualties.

Despite his brutality, Alexander was generous and respectful to his own fallen soldiers. After burying his dead near the Granicus, Alexander

The ruins of the majestic Parthenon, a temple dedicated to the goddess Athena, atop Athens's central hill, the Acropolis.

paid tribute to the fallen Macedonians, and sent word back to Pella that their families would no longer have to pay taxes. In particular, he singled out the twenty-five Companion horsemen who had died. Alexander hired the sculptor Lysippus to create bronze statues of them. These stood in the Macedonian town of Dium for nearly two centuries before being carted away by Roman invaders. Alexander also thanked the war goddess Athena for the victory by sending three-hundred sets of Persian armor to her temples on Athens's Acropolis. An inscription beside them read: "Alexander, son of Philip, and the Greeks. . . dedicate these spoils, taken from the Persians who dwell in Asia."

Following his major victory at the Granicus, Alexander continued on toward Ionia, leaving many more casualties in his wake. The leader of the important Ionian city of Miletus was unsure which side to back in the war, so he offered to open the city to both Macedonians and Persians. Alexander rejected this idea as an insult and brought up huge battering rams, which pounded the city's walls. When his soldiers finally broke in, many Milesians were killed. Three hundred men, probably Greek mercenaries, escaped and swam to a nearby island. When Alexander saw them preparing to fight to the death, like the members of the Theban Sacred Band, he decided that they would make good additions to his army and spared them.

At the next major Ionian city, Halicarnassus (about one hundred miles south of Ephesus), Alexander found Memnon and a Persian named Orontobates in charge. King Darius had recently given Memnon full command of the Persian provinces in Asia Minor. Alexander unleashed siege towers and battering rams and had his men dig saps (tunnels) under the walls. "The catapults mounted on [the] towers kept up a continuous pressure by hurling heavy stones," Arrian says. "Javelins flew thick and fast, and the defenders of the town were. . . beaten back," with heavy losses. As a result, Memnon abandoned the town and took refuge in a nearby fortress. Anxious to continue his march into Persian territory, Alexander decided not to stay and pursue the siege. He left that task to one of his chief deputies, Ptolemy, and departed with the bulk of the army.

Alexander next made his way to Gordium (or Gordion), in Phrygia, in central Asia Minor. It had a famous attraction—a huge, complicated knot tied around the shaft of an oxcart. A local legend claimed that whoever could undo the knot would become king of all Asia. Hearing that many people had tried and failed to unravel it, Alexander accepted the challenge. Some an-

AN INSCRIPTION BESIDE THEM READ:

"ALEXANDER, SON OF PHILIP, AND THE GREEKS. . . **DEDICATE THESE SPOILS,** TAKEN FROM THE PERSIANS WHO DWELL IN ASIA."

Alexander cutting the Gordian Knot by Jean Andre Castaigne (1898-1899)

cient accounts say he pulled out his sword and sliced the knot in half; others contend that he removed a wooden peg that held the knot to the shaft. Whatever method Alexander used, Arrian writes, "when he and his attendants left the place where the wagon stood, the general feeling was that the oracle [prophecy] about the untying of the knot had been fulfilled."

It was about the time that Alexander left Gordium that important news came. Memnon had escaped from Halicarnassus. But after trying to organize some anti-Macedonian rebellions in the Aegean islands, he had contracted a disease and died. Alexander immediately grasped that this was a crucial turning point and opportunity for him. Darius now lacked a strong general in the western part of his empire, which meant that he would be forced to take the field himself against the invaders. Excited by this prospect, Alexander pushed his men onward, eager for a new date with destiny.

A 1529 painting of *The Battle of Issus* by Altdorfer Albrecht

CHAPTER FIVE

FROM
DESTROYER TO
LIBERATOR

A s Alexander made his way through Asia Minor, his overall strategy for the coming months was clear. Ultimately, of course, he intended to invade the Persian heartland, which lay in Mesopotamia and the Iranian Plateau. There, he planned to capture the Persian capitals of Babylon, Susa, and Persepolis. But before he could do this, he needed to subdue Darius's western holdings, including Asia Minor, Syria, Palestine, and Egypt. Only after securing these lands would Alexander feel confident in driving farther eastward into Asia.

Considering these strategic factors, Alexander was encouraged to hear that Darius was moving westward, hoping to intercept him near the Mediterranean coast. The Persian king had gathered an army several times larger than the Macedonian one. And apparently his royal advisors had convinced him that Alexander would be so frightened by this great battalion that he would flee rather than fight. According to Arrian, even if Alexander did decide to fight, the advisors claimed, "the Persian cavalry would ride over the Macedonian army and trample it to pieces." Darius accepted this advice, Arrian says, because he "was always ready to believe what he found it most agreeable to believe."

These were grave miscalculations, however. Alexander was neither awed nor rattled by enemy numbers greater than his own. Ever since Xe-

Alexander as he appears in the famous "Alexander Mosaic," depicting the battle of Issus. The mosaic now rests in the Naples National Archaeological Museum. (*Courtesy StockImages/Alamy*)

rxes' invasion of Greece in the fifth century BC, Greek armies had repeatedly proven superior to the Persians in battle. Moreover, Alexander believed that he had the finest army Greece had ever fielded. "We of Macedon for generations past have been trained in the hard school of danger and war," he told his officers, according to Arrian. And his Greek allies "are the best and stoutest soldiers in Europe." Alexander was therefore very confident of victory. He reasoned that a decisive win over Darius so early in the campaign would send a wave of fear across Asia, increasing the odds of Persia's defeat.

The initial clash between Alexander and Darius took place in November 333 BC Having crossed the Euphrates River in northern Mesopotamia, Darius reached Sochi, near the Mediterranean coast. Meanwhile, Alexander descended from Asia Minor into Syria. As the two armies searched for a favorable spot to fight, they unknowingly passed each other on opposite sides of a mountain range. So when they finally met, at Issus in northern Syria, Darius's forces faced south and Alexander's north.

Now that the opposing armies could see each other, the huge disparity in their sizes became clear. The figure of 600,000 reported for Darius's forces by several ancient historians is not credible. Organizing, equipping, and feeding that many soldiers on such short notice was beyond the capabilities of any

A detail of Albrecht's *The Battle of Issus*

ancient king, including Darius. Furthermore, such a force could not have fit, much less maneuvered, in any of Syria's small coastal plains, where Darius planned to engage Alexander.

The Persian army was nevertheless quite large. Reliable modern estimates suggest that Darius had two divisions of infantry—some 60,000 Persian foot soldiers called Kardakes; and between 10,000 and 30,000 Greek mercenary hoplites. There were also between 20,000 and 30,000 Persian cavalry. Thus Darius had somewhere between 90,000 and 120,000 fighters, compared to Alexander's combined infantry and cavalry of only 30,000.

In spite of the superior Persian numbers, Darius was at an immediate disadvantage. The Issus plain was not wide enough for him to deploy all of his men effectively; many had to be stationed well behind the front lines or in nearby foothills. Alexander quickly exploited the situation. He sent some of his light-armed foot soldiers into the hills, where they drove away the Persians in that area, robbing Darius of their use.

Then Alexander initiated the main battle by leading the Companion Cavalry on his right wing in a furious assault on the Persians' left wing. "The

Persian left collapsed the very moment he was on them," wrote Arrian. But as the Companions rapidly pushed the opposing horsemen backwards, Alexander's center had a more difficult time. Encountering some rough terrain, the phalanx was unable to maintain its unbroken front wall of pikes. Darius's Greeks exploited gaps in that wall.

However, Alexander and his horsemen soon remedied this situation. They "swung left towards the center [and] delivered a flank attack on the [Greek] mercenaries and were soon cutting them to pieces," Arrian wrote. As the tide of battle turned, Alexander spotted Darius on his chariot a few hundred yards away and rode straight for him. Terrified, the Persian king jumped from the vehicle, mounted a horse, and fled the field. Not long afterward, most of the other Persians did the same.

The casualty figures for Issus are uncertain. The number of Persian dead given by Arrian, Plutarch, and Diodorus—100,000 or more—is almost certainly an exaggeration. It is important to remember that their works were written centuries after the event and based on Macedonian accounts, which were likely biased and exaggerated. Still, Darius's losses may well have been in the tens of thousands. Alexander and his troops pursued the fleeing enemy for miles, killing more opponents after the battle than during it.

Alexander's victory at Issus had several dimensions. Besides significantly reducing Persia's effective armed forces, the invaders had shamed the Persian king, winning a major propaganda coup. The victory also allowed Alexander to seize an enormous treasury of gold and silver Darius had stored in Syria. This loot alone was enough to finance an enormous military expedition for many years. In addition, when he overran the Persian camp near Issus, Alexander took into custody Darius's mother, wife, and children.

The young conqueror treated these captives with great respect and kindness. He realized that holding onto them would give him considerable leverage over his enemy. Indeed, Darius soon demonstrated the weak position he was in by offering peace, friendship, and even part of his empire in exchange for the royal prisoners. Arrian's account says that one of the letters Darius sent to Alexander read in part:

> Alexander has sent no representative to [my] court to confirm the former friendship and alliance between the two kingdoms; on the contrary, he has crossed into Asia with his armed forces and

Painter Dudley Tennant's depiction of the battle of Issus
(Courtesy of Classic Image/Alamy)

done much damage to the Persians. For this reason [I] took the field in defense of [my] country and of [my] ancestral throne. The issue of the battle was as some god willed. Now Darius the King asks Alexander the King to restore from captivity his wife, his mother, and his children, and is willing to make friends with him and be his ally. For this cause [I] urge Alexander to send to [me]. . . representatives of his own in order that proper guarantees may be exchanged.

Alexander's curt reply, in Arrian's account, reveals the arrogance, extreme confidence, and unwillingness to compromise that so often marked his character:

Your ancestors invaded Macedonia and Greece and caused havoc in our country, though we had done nothing to provoke them. As supreme commander of all Greece, I invaded Asia because I wished to punish Persia for this act, an act which must be laid wholly to your charge. . ... Now I have defeated yourself and the army you led. By God's help I am master of your country. . . . Come to me, therefore, as you would come to the lord of the continent of Asia. . . . And in the future let any communication you wish to make with me be addressed to the King of all Asia. Do not write to me as an equal. Everything you possess is now mine; so if you should want anything, let me know in the proper terms, or I shall take steps to deal with you as a criminal. If, on the other hand, you wish to dispute your throne, stand and fight for it and do not run away. Wherever you may hide yourself, be sure I shall seek you out.

At some point during Alexander's continued march down the Mediterranean coast into Palestine, important news came from Greece. In his absence, a Persian fleet had attempted to seize control of the Hellespont and cut off one of his main supply routes. But Alexander's own fleet, commanded by his able generals Hegelochus and Amphoterus, had removed this threat.

The success of this rear-guard operation allowed Alexander to give his full attention to bringing the Phoenician cities (in what are now Lebanon, Syria, Israel and the Palestinian territories) into his growing empire. News of his major victories at the Granicus and Issus preceded him. One by one the Phoenician strongholds, including Byblos and Sidon, welcomed him without resistance. These cities were not only famous trade depots that handled goods from across Europe, North Africa, and Asia, but also key naval bases for the Persian fleet. Now that they were in Alexander's hands, that fleet could no longer operate effectively. Darius was left only with his remaining land forces.

Up until the end of 333 BC, Alexander had enjoyed an amazingly swift march through more than a thousand miles of enemy territory. This satisfied his pressing desire to conquer as many lands as he could in the shortest possible time. But to his utter frustration, an unexpected obstacle now forced him to slow down. The next large Phoenician city after Sidon—Tyre—put up a stiff fight. When Alexander first met with the city's leaders, they said they would consider some sort of peace deal. However, they would not allow him or his men to enter their city. To Alexander, this was unacceptable insolence. In his view, the city had only two choices—to cooperate by choice or to do so by force. He began laying siege to Tyre.

The main part of the city had been built on a small island about half a mile offshore. Alexander decided to build an artificial mole, or stone break-water, from the mainland to the island. When Tyrian ships began harassing his workers, he had towers built on the mole. These were covered in animal hides to protect the workers. Alexander also placed catapults and archers in the towers to shower the enemy ships with missiles. Countering this, the Tyrians sent in fire-ships, which collided with and burned the towers. Next, Alexander collected large numbers of Phoenician ships from Sidon and elsewhere and sent them against the town. But it was extremely well fortified and difficult to capture, as Arrian explains:

A naval assault during the siege of Tyre

> On the battlements overlooking the mole, the Tyrians erected wooden towers for defensive action, and every threat from Alexander. . . they met with missile weapons, using fire arrows against the ships with such effect that their crews were afraid to approach within range. The walls of the town opposite the mole were [very] high [and] strongly built of large stone blocks cemented together. [Also] blocks of stone in large numbers had been thrown into the water and obstructed [the] advance [of Alexander's ships].

Thanks to these stout defenses, along with the Tyrians' stubbornness and courage, the city held out for an incredible seven months. But during this period Alexander's ships and troops kept up relentless assaults. Eventually the attackers managed to open a breach in Tyre's outer wall, and over several days he gap widened. Alexander finally entered the town with some of his best

The Tyrians' Last Stand

This gripping excerpt from Arrian's biography of Alexander describes the Tyrians' last stand after the Macedonians had broken into the city:

> The main body of the Tyrian defenders abandoned the wall once they saw it was in the enemy's hands, and withdrew to the shrine of Agenor [a building honoring the city's mythical founder], where they turned to face the Macedonians. Alexander and the [Hypaspists] were soon upon them. Some fell fighting, others fled, with Alexander in pursuit. . . . The slaughter was terrible, for the Macedonians, sick as they were of the length of the siege, went to work with savage ferocity.

A 1696 engraving of the siege of Tyre by Alexander

men, including the Hypaspists. In the bloody massacre that followed, about 8,000 Tyrians were slain (compared to roughly four hundred Macedonians) and Alexander sold the other 30,000 inhabitants into slavery.

After Tyre's fall in the late summer of 332 BC, Alexander pushed on to Gaza, in southern Palestine. In spite of the brutal example he had made of Tyre, the people of Gaza decided to fight rather than submit. This time, though, the siege was relatively brief. Gaza was considerably easier to capture because it was located on the mainland rather than an island. Alexander had his men dig tunnels under the city's walls and use tall ladders to scale the battlements. Almost all the male inhabitants of Gaza died in a brave but futile defense; the women and children ended up in slave markets.

Alexander visits an Egyptian temple in Memphis in this engraving by Jean Andre Castaigne

With Gaza secured, the way was now open for the Macedonians and other Greeks to enter Egypt. That once mighty kingdom had been under Persian rule off and on for almost two centuries. And the Egyptians hated the Persians with a passion. So when Alexander arrived in the Egyptian cities of Pelusium, Heliopolis, and Memphis, the locals welcomed him as a liberator. He then proceeded to foster even more good will by worshiping at the temples of their gods.

The most famous religious shrine Alexander visited in Egypt was that of the ancient god Ammon-Re. (Worship of this god had spread to Greece in the prior century; so Alexander was already familiar with Ammon's cult.) Located in the oasis of Siwa, in eastern Libya, the shrine was famous for its oracle, a priest who was said to convey the god's words to humans. According to Plutarch, Alexander asked Ammon whether he, Alexander, "was

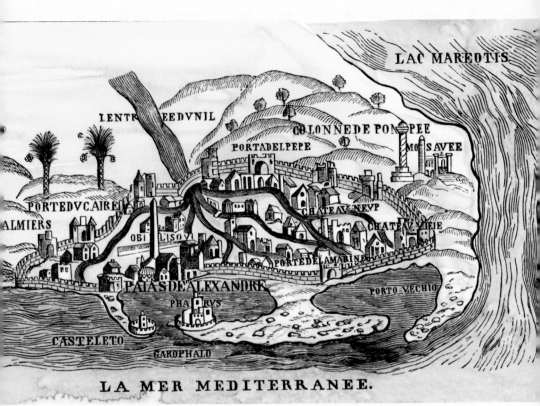

Alexandria in the 1500s. By that time Pharos (in foreground) was connected to the mainland. *(Courtesy of North Wind Picture Archives / Alamy).*

destined to rule over all mankind. This, the god replied, would be granted
to him." The young king then "dedicated some magnificent offerings to the
god and presented large sums of money to his priests." Another ancient story
claims that these priests hailed the royal visitor as the son of Zeus, whom
both the Egyptians and Greeks identified with Ammon.

An act of more lasting importance that Alexander performed while
in Egypt was the founding of a major new city. Dubbed Alexandria, in his
own honor, it was destined to quickly grow into one of the chief commercial
and cultural centers of the ancient world. Alexander chose a site on the
Mediterranean coast in the Nile Delta, near the tiny island of Pharos. "When

DECIDING ALEXANDRIA'S LAYOUT

According to several ancient sources, Alexander aided Deinocrates in deciding the basic layout of Alexandria, although the mention of divine signs makes this story sound suspiciously like a fable added after the fact. As Plutarch tells it:

> There was no chalk to mark the ground plan, so they took barley meal, sprinkled it on the dark earth, and marked out a semi-circle, which was divided into equal segments by lines radiating from the inner arc to the circumference. The shape was similar to that of a chlamys, or military cloak . . . . While the king was enjoying the symmetry of the design, suddenly huge flocks of birds appeared from the river and the lagoon, descended upon the site, and devoured every grain of the barley. Alexander was greatly disturbed by this omen, but the diviners urged him to take heart and [claimed it was] a sign that the city would not only have abundant resources of its own, but would be the nurse of men of innumerable nations, and so he ordered those in charge of the work to proceed.

he saw what wonderful natural advantages the place possessed," Plutarch writes, including a "spacious harbor," he "ordered the plan of the city to be designed." For this important job, Alexander chose a well-known Greek architect, Deinocrates, a native of Rhodes.

Alexander did not stay to see the first buildings rise on the site. Restless as always to move on to the next adventure, he left Egypt and made his way back into southern Palestine. His conquest of the Mediterranean seaboard complete, it was now time to head eastward for the long-awaited assault on Persia's heartland.

Marble bust of Alexander
(Courtesy of Roget Cracknell 01/classic/Alamy)

CHAPTER SIX

TO BE
MASTER OF
ALL ASIA

In the early months of 331 BC, Alexander collected several thousand reinforcements in preparation for the main thrust of his anti-Persian campaign, increasing the strength of his foot soldiers to about 40,000. That included the pikemen of the phalanx, the Hypaspists, some Greek hoplites, and several units of archers and other light-armed fighters. He also had some 7,000 horsemen, including the Macedonian Companions, the Thessalians, and other allied Greek cavalry units. With this refurbished army he departed Palestine in July and marched eastward into the plains of Mesopotamia.

As Alexander neared the Euphrates River, his scouts reported that a small force of Persian troops was guarding the far bank. The Persian commander, Mazaeus, had about 3,000 cavalry and 2,000 Greek mercenary hoplites. Seeing that he had no chance against the advancing army, Mazaeus withdrew and headed eastward. He may have hoped that Alexander would give chase. That would have both stretched the Macedonian supply lines thin and drawn the invaders away from the Persian heartland.

However, Alexander did not take the bait. In his mind, there was no time to lose in confronting Darius, who had reportedly been collecting troops for a last stand in northern Mesopotamia. The Macedonians hastily erected two pontoon bridges on the Euphrates and crossed over without incident. (A pontoon bridge consists of a walkway laid over a row of floating barges or boats.) When Alexander and his men reached the other great Mesopotamian river, the Tigris, however, the crossing was much harder. This was because the Tigris's currents were considerably stronger and faster than those of the Euphrates. According to Diodorus,

> [The crossing] was accomplished not only with difficulty but even at substantial risk. The depth of the water at the ford [chosen for the crossing] was above a man's breast and the force of the current swept away many who were crossing and deprived them of their footing, and as the water struck their shields, it bore many off their course and brought them into extreme danger. But Alexander contrived a defense against the violence of the river. He ordered all to lock arms with each other and to construct a sort of bridge out of the compact union of their persons.

The crossing exhausted the men. And though Alexander was as usual eager to press on, as Arrian says, "once over the river, he gave his men a rest."

In late September, four days after crossing the Tigris, Alexander's scouts arrived at a gallop with important news. A large Persian army lay only a few miles away on a wide plain near the small village of Gaugamela.

Darius had gathered soldiers from all corners of his vast empire. The exact size of this army is unknown, but there were likely about 30,000 to 35,000 cavalry, outnumbering Alexander's horsemen four or five to one. Many of Darius's riders wore mail, a flexible kind of armor consisting of rows of thin metal scales sewn or glued to a leather or cloth jerkin. The Persian army also boasted some 6,000 Greek mercenary infantry.

The rest of Darius's motley forces included a mix of unarmored cavalry, archers, and other light-armed troops. By modern estimates, the total Persian forces came to between 90,000 and 100,000 soldiers, along with two hundred battle chariots. The latter were equipped with sharpened metal blades protruding sideways from the wheel hubs; the drivers planned to maneuver close to the enemy infantry and slice them to ribbons.

Darius knew that Alexander was fast approaching from the west. So

This eighteenth-century ivory relief of the Battle of Gaugamela is on display at the National Archaelogical Museum of Spain.

the Persian monarch ordered his huge array of soldiers to assume their battle formations, which stretched for miles across the plain. Alexander did not oblige his adversary by attacking right away, however. Instead, the Macedonians and their allies made camp a few miles from the plain.

Worried that Alexander might launch a sudden night attack, Darius told his men to stay in their ranks on the battlefield. So while the Macedonians had a good meal and enjoyed some sleep that night, the Persians got little or no rest. According to the Roman historian Curtius's account, Darius made the rounds of the field, doing his best to raise his men's spirits:

He called upon [the gods] to inspire the men with a courage in keeping with their glory of old and their forefathers' monumental achievements. . . . The gods were certainly on their side. They had recently struck a sudden panic into the Macedonians, he added, who were still in a state of distracted fear. . . . Nor was their leader [Alexander] any saner. . . . Like a beast of the wild, he was totally preoccupied with the plunder he was seeking and charging straight into [a] trap.

It may well be that Darius thought he had Alexander trapped. In the morning, as the Macedonians prepared for battle, Alexander saw that the Persian lines stretched as far as the eye could see toward both the left and right. He lacked the troop strength to create an opposing line of equal length. So he positioned each of his wings at an angle, with the front lines facing the far left and far right. That way it would be more difficult for the enemy to execute a flanking maneuver, enveloping his sides. On the chance that he was outflanked, he also sent a unit of infantry to guard his rear.

For an undetermined number of minutes the opposing combatants eyed each other in nervous silence. Then Alexander opened the conflict by leading his right-wing Companion horsemen forward and toward the right. Instead of charging straight at the enemy, however, they rode farther and farther sideways toward the right.

Meanwhile, Darius initiated his own action by ordering his chariots forward toward the phalanx's closely packed mass of men and iron. The Macedonian pikemen were ready for this move, however, thanks to special instructions Alexander had given them. "As the phalanx joined shields," Diodorus says, "all beat upon their shields with their spears as the king had commanded, and a great din arose. As the [frightened Persian] horses shied off, most of the chariots were turned about. . . . Others continued on against the Macedonian lines, but as the soldiers opened wide gaps in their ranks, the chariots were channeled through these [openings]." Once the vehicles had passed through, the ranks closed back up and men with javelins slew the horses and charioteers from a safe distance.

By this time, Alexander and his Companions had moved far to the right of their original position. Seeing this, Darius must have figured that his opponent was trying to outflank his left wing. So the Persian king ordered troops from his center to reinforce his left. Little by little, exactly as Alexander had hoped, this caused a gap to form in the Persian center. When he felt the time was right, he suddenly turned and led his cavalry through this gap. The phalanx followed. And as had occurred at Issus, Alexander eventually found and made his way straight toward Darius. According to Plutarch:

> Darius was a tall and handsome man and he towered conspicuously above this large and superbly equipped body of horsemen, who were closely massed to guard the lofty chariot in which he stood. But the horseguards were seized with panic at the terrible sight of Alexander bearing down upon them. . . and the greater number of them broke and scattered. . . . As for Darius, all the horrors of the battle were now before his eyes. The forces which had been stationed in the center for his protection had now been driven back upon him; it had become difficult to turn his chariot round and drive it away. . . . In this [predicament] the king abandoned his chariot and his armor, mounted a mare. . . and rode away.

The Alexander Mosaic, showing the battle of Issus

The battle was not yet over, however. Although Alexander and the Companions enjoyed success in the center, some Persian cavalry units managed to penetrate the Macedonian ranks. Several minutes later they attacked Alexander's baggage train on the far edge of the plain. They did considerable damage before the infantrymen guarding the Macedonian rear caught up and drove them away. Another intrepid group of Persians attacked the Macedonian left, commanded by Parmenio. But they were soon trapped between Parmenio and Alexander, who had swung around toward their rear. For these Persians, according to Arrian, "it was every man for himself, struggling to break through as if in that alone lay his hope of life." Finally, in desperation, those Persians who had not already fled the field did so in a headlong rout.

The battle of Gaugamela had proven a great disaster for both Darius and his empire. The Persian king was in flight. And fear and chaos swirled in his wake, for his army had been shattered. Casualty figures given by Arrian, Diodorus, and other ancient historians vary from as few as 40,000 to as many as 300,000 Persians killed in the battle. The number of Macedonians slain is usually given as five hundred or fewer.

Although those casualty figures remain uncertain, there is no doubt that Alexander's victory was overwhelming; it ended all credible opposition to his capture of the Persian Empire. Indeed, soon after the great battle, Alexander's men proclaimed him "master of all Asia." This took place at Arbela, about seventy-five miles from Gaugamela. Alexander had hurried to Arbela in hopes of finding Darius there. But the defeated monarch was already gone. Accompanied by a small contingent of bodyguards and soldiers, he had headed eastward toward Media, the hilly country now occupied by north-central Iran.

Alexander fully intended to continue his pursuit of Darius. But for the moment the need to gain firm control over Persia's capitals appeared more pressing. The closest of these cities was Babylon. Mazaeus, the Persian general whom the Macedonians had encountered near the Euphrates, had taken charge of this huge and splendid metropolis. He now prudently rode out to meet the approaching Alexander. After surrendering Babylon, Mazaeus accompanied the Macedonian leaders into the city, which gave them a big and festive welcome. "A large number of the Babylonians had taken up a position on the walls," Curtius wrote, "eager to have a view of their new king. [The] man in charge of the [city's defenses] and royal trea-

A 1664 oil painting of Alexander's entry into Babylon
by Charles Le Brun

SOON AFTER THE GREAT BATTLE,
ALEXANDER'S MEN
PROCLAIMED HIM
"MASTER OF
ALL ASIA."
THIS TOOK PLACE AT ARBELA, ABOUT
SEVENTY-FIVE MILES FROM GAUGAMELA.

sury. . . had carpeted the whole road with flowers and garlands and set up at intervals on both sides silver altars heaped. . . with [spices and] perfumes. Following him were his gifts [for Alexander]—herds of cattle and horses, [along with priests] chanting a song [and] musicians."

Having taken Babylon without a fight, Alexander appointed a number of Macedonians and Greeks to various civil and financial posts there. This surprised no one. It was routine for ancient conquerors to place their own followers in charge of the peoples and cities they had defeated. What Alexander did next, however, was completely unexpected by both the Greeks and Persians. He made his former enemy Mazaeus governor of Babylon and its surrounding territories.

There may have been some grumbling among Alexander's deputies over the appointment of Mazaeus, but they soon saw its wisdom. Hearing about such lenient treatment of Persian officials, other satraps hastened to submit peacefully. Abulites, governor of Susa (situated east of the Tigris River in southwestern Iran), soon surrendered to and welcomed the Macedonians. Alexander allowed Abulites to remain in his post. Also at Susa,

The ruins of Persepolis

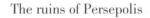

Alexander acquired a rich cache of silver, further increasing his fortune and allowing him to continue funding his campaign.

Alexander next marched on the principal Persian capital, Persepolis, located north of the Persian Gulf in southern Iran. (The Persians called it Parsa; Persepolis was its Greek name, based on words meaning "Persian city.") He hoped that it, like many other Persian cities, would fall to him without resistance and the loss of Macedonian lives. But this was not to be. An estimated 25,000 Persians had gathered in the so-called "Persian Gates," a mountain pass located not far west of Persepolis. In a last gesture of patriotism and defiance, they hoped to deny the invaders access to their most beloved city.

Alexander decided to take the pass using stealth tactics. First he made camp near its western end. Then, leaving his officer Craterus in charge, in the middle of the night the king led a large contingent of troops around the mountain and by dawn made it to the other side of the pass. At a trumpet signal, Alexander attacked from the west while Craterus did so from the east, thereby trapping the Persians. According to Arrian:

> The Macedonians were all around them. . . . Most of [the Persians] had no option but to turn back to the inner defenses [likely some makeshift stone walls] in the hope of saving themselves there. But these defenses, too, were already in Macedonian hands. . . . In some close fighting [the Persians were cut] to pieces. A few escaped, but in their desperate efforts to avoid destruction, leapt to their death over the edge of the cliffs.

After the slaughter, Alexander wasted no time. While the bulk of his troops proceeded at a comfortable pace, he raced onward at top speed with his Companions. Arriving in Persepolis ahead of the news of the fateful battle, he swiftly seized the royal palaces and another of Darius's large treasure troves. Parmenio urged Alexander to spare the palaces, which rested on a gigantic raised stone terrace overlooking the city. The argument was that this would foster goodwill among the local Persians. But Alexander reportedly wanted to burn the royal buildings to avenge Xerxes' burning of Athens in the preceding century. Some ancient accounts claim that Alexander started the fire after getting drunk at a party. But many modern scholars think this story was fabricated later. In whatever manner the inferno began, the damage it did is still visible in the buildings' stately ruins.

Having secured most of Persia's leading cities, in the early summer of 330 BC, Alexander headed northward to resume his pursuit of Darius. The fugitive king may still have held out some hope of regaining his wife, children, and throne. But he had been unable to raise a significant force of troops. For him, the unpleasant truth was that large numbers of his satraps and other nobles, along with their followers, had submitted to Alexander.

Leaving Media, Darius fled eastward into what is now northeastern Iran. As Alexander followed, he received the stunning news that the man he was chasing had been taken prisoner by his own followers. The leading traitor was Bessus, satrap of the Persian province of Bactria (centered in what is now northern Afghanistan). He had declared himself Darius's successor and assumed the royal name of King Artaxerxes V. The plan was to keep the former monarch in chains as an insurance policy. If Alexander managed to catch up, the conspirators reasoned, they would trade Darius in exchange for their lives.

That day of reckoning came sooner than Bessus and the others could have imagined. On hearing about Darius's capture, Alexander gathered five hundred of his best men and rode day and night through the hot, dusty Iranian hills. Bessus and his accomplices got word that the Macedonians were closing in on them. And in a panic, they ran Darius through with their spears and fled.

Not long afterward, one of Alexander's soldiers, Polystratus, appeared on the scene. As he stopped to drink from a stream, he saw an abandoned wagon nearby and heard a man moaning. Hurrying over, he discovered Darius, still chained, with the spears protruding from his torso. The once mighty ruler of the world's largest empire lay near death, alone except for his faithful dog. Polystratus gave the man some water and tried to keep him alive. But Darius passed away before Alexander arrived a few minutes later. Seeing his former adversary's pathetic remains, the Macedonian king covered the body with his own cloak and vowed to apprehend the murderers. Clearly, Persia's conquest would not be complete until the usurper and his distant domain of Bactria were in Alexander's grasp.

DARIUS'S LAST WORDS

In his biography of Alexander, Plutarch claims that the dying Darius took Polystratus's hand and uttered these words: "This is the final stroke of misfortune, that I should accept a service from you, and not be able to return it. But Alexander will reward you for your kindness, and the gods will repay him for his courtesy towards my mother and my wife and my children. And so through you, I give him my hand."

In this romanticized illustration by French artist Gustave Dore, Alexander discovers the body of Darius, murdered by Bessus and his cronies.

A marble statue of Alexander
(Courtesy of Roget Cracknell 01/classic/Alamy)

CHAPTER SEVEN

ADVENTURES IN AFGHANISTAN

After Darius's death, Alexander saw himself poised at a major turning point in his kingship, military career, and life in general. In an amazingly brief span of time, he had brought the world's biggest empire to its knees. And he now faced having to make the crucial decision of what to do next. On the one hand, he recognized that he had acquired a major new responsibility: having conquered Persia, he had to rule it, an enormous and difficult task that only a handful of the many Persian monarchs had been able to do well.

On the other hand, Alexander felt compelled to push onward. Persia's remote eastern provinces had yet to be seized and absorbed into his new empire. Beyond their borders, moreover, even more distant lands beckoned. Some undefined primal urge or personal dream continued to drive him toward conquering as much of the known world as he could, while he could. Thus, at the age of twenty-six he undertook a dual challenge. He would rule his immense realm while simultaneously attempting to expand it. In hindsight, it is clear that even someone as smart, talented, and energetic as Alexander could not do both of these things indefinitely and well. And as he pursued new adventures in the wilds of what is now Afghanistan, he began to feel the strain of doing too much too fast.

Alexander worked hard at maintaining the loyalty of his subjects, but wasn't always successful. He certainly tried hard to gain the allegiance of the subjugated Persians. First, he buried Darius with high honors in an elaborate ceremony. He also spread the rumor that Darius's last wish had been for Alexander to bring his murderers to justice; accordingly, there was a concerted effort to find and punish Bessus and the other conspirators. In addition, Alexander continued to appoint Persians to important administrative posts, including provincial governor.

The Macedonian king even adopted a number of Persian customs, including wearing various kinds of traditional Persian attire at court. He surprised many people when he married Roxane, the daughter of a Persian nobleman. According to Plutarch, the marriage "played a great part in furthering his policy of reconciliation [with the conquered Persians]. The barbarians were encouraged by the feeling of partnership which [the marriage] created, and they were completely won over by Alexander's moderation and courtesy."

But with so much of his energy spent on pleasing his new subjects, Alexander sometimes had a harder time appeasing his fellow Greeks. Having been away from their homeland and families for four years, many of his soldiers were war-weary and restless. They also did not like his elevation of Persians, rather than Macedonians, to high government posts; nor were they happy to see their leader donning Persian clothing. A number of Alexander's men were also disturbed by his choosing a Persian wife. They objected to the idea that any male child produced by the union—the successor to the throne—would be a non-Greek.

Still another complaint that circulated among Alexander's men was his sudden demand that they, and everyone else, adopt the Persian custom of *proskynesis* at court. It consisted of a person prostrating himself or herself—lying face down on the floor—before the king. The Greeks viewed such groveling as demeaning and unworthy of a free person. Arrian's account cites an episode in which one of Alexander's officers, Callisthenes, boldly protested imposing such prostration on the Macedonians and Greeks. "I beg you, Alexander, to remember Greece," Callisthenes said. "When you are home again, do you really propose to force the Greeks, who love their liberty more than anyone else in the world, to prostrate themselves before you?" Callisthenes also objected to *proskynesis* on religious grounds:

An engraving of the wedding of Alexander and the Persian maiden
Roxanne by Jean Andre Castaigne

WE OUGHT NOT TO MAKE A MAN LOOK BIGGER THAN HE IS BY PAYING HIM EXCESSIVE AND EXTRAVAGANT HONOR, OR. . . [BY] PUTTING [THE GODS] ON THE SAME LEVEL AS MEN.

For my part, I hold Alexander fit for any mark of honor that a man may earn. But do not forget that there is a difference between honoring a man and worshipping a god. The distinction between the two has been marked in many ways. . ... Yet of all these things not one is so important as this very custom of prostration. Men greet each other with a kiss; but a god, far above us on his mysterious throne, it is not lawful for us to touch—and that is why we [pay] homage [by] bowing to the earth before him. . . . It is wrong, therefore, to ignore these distinctions; we ought not to make a man look bigger than he is by paying him excessive and extravagant honor, or . . . [by] putting [the gods] on the same level as men.

Alexander soon realized how unpopular the new rule would be and decided not to impose it after all. Increasing displeasure among some of Alexander's followers led to secret resistance to his policies and a number of plots against his life. The most celebrated case occurred in October 330 BC, only a few months after Darius's death and funeral. It came to light that a Macedonian soldier named Dimnus was involved in a conspiracy against the king. After his arrest he named other conspirators. Among them was Philotus, commander of the Companion Cavalry and one of the three sons of Alexander's leading general, Parmenio.

Hearing of the charge against Philotus, Alexander followed Macedonian custom by convening a group of Companions to ask for their advice. They called for a trial. Philotus and several others named in the plot were arrested. The next day, selected members of the Companions, Hypaspists, and phalanx met in what the Macedonians called a "people's court." After hearing the testimony of witnesses, they would decide on the verdict. "The persons who had reported the affair came forward," Arrian says, "with various irrefutable proofs of his [Philotus's] own guilt and that of his fellow conspirators, of which the most damning was that he admitted knowledge of a plot against Alexander but had said nothing about it, in spite of the fact that he was in the habit of visiting Alexander's tent twice a day."

Philotus and the other conspirators were found guilty. Following Macedonian custom, they were immediately executed by a shower of javelins unleashed by the assembled soldiers. Moreover, Alexander decided to rid himself of Philotus's father, on the chance that he, too, had known about the plot. Arrian continues:

> The reason for Parmenio's execution may have been that Alexander could not believe that he had no share in his son's conspiracy. On the other hand, even granting his innocence, his living on after his son's execution was already in fact a danger. For he was a man of immense prestige. He had great influence not only with Alexander himself, but also with the army, and not alone with the Macedonian units, but also with the mercenary soldiers.

Whatever the reasons may have been, Alexander sent soldiers to Media, where Parmenio was then stationed. They stabbed the aging general to death while he was still reading the charges against him.

Dealing with administrative matters and court intrigues occupied only a few weeks of Alexander's time. A military opportunist to the core, he felt the urge to press onward to new strategies and conquests. Late in 330

BC he passed through southwestern Bactria. Then he followed the Helmond River valley to the Persian satrapy of Arachosia (in what is now southeastern Afghanistan). There, he established a new town, calling it Alexandria-in-Arachosia.

Alexander could have proceeded farther eastward. But at this point he preferred, as he so often did, to secure his rear. Bessus was still on the loose in Bactria and might be raising troops who could potentially threaten Macedonian supply lines.

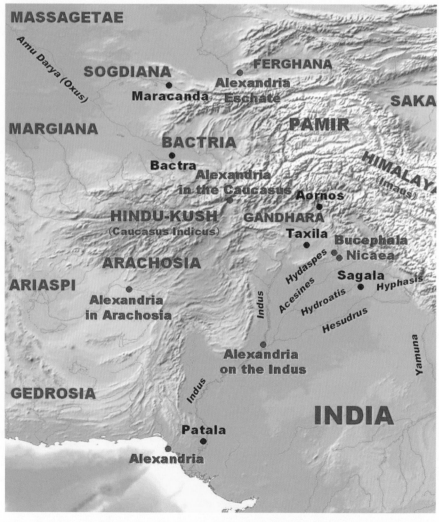

The red cities were founded by Alexander.

Early in 329 BC, Alexander reached the Bactrian city of Kunduz. There, word came that some of Bessus's own followers had arrested him and had decided to hand him over to Alexander. Not long afterward, some of Alexander's men found Bessus on a roadway, stripped naked, chained, and wearing a dog collar. (His captors had already fled, fearful of what the Macedonians might do to them.)

After denouncing the bound man, Alexander sent him back to Media to be dealt with by Darius's still grieving relatives. They first mercilessly tortured the usurper. Then, as described by Plutarch, they "had the tops of two straight trees bent down so that they met, and part of Bessus' body was tied to each; then, when each tree was let go, and sprang back to its upright position, the part of the body attached to it was torn off by the recoil."

From central Bactria, Alexander marched farther northward into the Persian province of Sogdiana. Located between the Oxus and Jaxartes rivers (in modern Uzbekistan), it oversaw lucrative trade routes passing through south-central Asia. Here, the Macedonians encountered a foe considerably more formidable than Darius. That opponent was a Bactrian-born Sogdian named Spitamenes. In organizing local resistance to Alexander, Spitamenes also gathered as his allies tribesmen from Scythia, the region lying north of the Jaxartes. The Sogdians and Scythians proved skilled at guerilla warfare. And for almost three years they bogged Alexander down in a series of skirmishes and ambushes. More Macedonians and Greeks died in these small engagements than fell at the Granicus, Issus, and Gaugamela combined.

In the person of Spitamenes, Alexander faced a smart and tough opponent. This passage from Arrian's account describes how the Sogdian wiped out a unit of Macedonians commanded by Pharnuches.

> He [Spitamenes] dispatched his cavalry to gallop round the Macedonian infantry formations, discharging their arrows as they rode. Pharnuches' men attempted to charge, but to no purpose. The enemy, on their sifter horses, were out of range in a moment. . . . The Macedonians tried now to stand their ground, now to withdraw, but all to no effect. In either case, the weight of the Scythian cavalry was too much for them. [The Macedonian horsemen] attempted to cross the river [and] the infantry without orders promptly followed suit, scrambling down the steep bank into the

water in a panic. . . . Showers of [Scythian] arrows were poured in. The Macedonians were helpless, and all who survived took refuge on a small island in the river. But this did not save them, for Spitamenes' cavalry and the Scythians surrounded the island and shot them down to a man. The few prisoners taken were promptly butchered.

A 1696 engraving of the head of Spitamenes, being presented to Alexander

Eventually, the threat posed by Spitamenes ended. He allied himself with a particularly fierce Scythian tribe, the Massagetae, and they continued to attack small units of Macedonians and Greeks patrolling the region. At some point in the winter of 328 BC, however, a false rumor spread that Alexander was moving against the Massagetae with his whole army. Desiring to avoid such a confrontation, the commander of the Massagetae turned on and killed Spitamenes. Alexander soon received the latter's head as a peace offering.

Alexander's joy at hearing of Spitamenes' demise was tempered to some degree by the death of a close friend. Moreover, this loss was magnified by the fact that the king himself performed the deed. Earlier that winter, Alexander had appointed Cleitus, the man who had saved his life at the Granicus, to the post of satrap of Bactria and Sogdiana. (Alexander had decided to combine the two provinces into one.) At a party attended by Alexander and several of his officers, a singer started to recite verses that ridiculed some recently fallen Macedonian soldiers. And some of those present, including Cleitus, took extreme offense. But the king, who was quite drunk, ordered the singer to continue.

Finally, Cleitus, who had also had much to drink, was unable to contain himself any longer. He lashed out at Alexander, as recalled by Plutarch:

> [Cleitus] shouted that it was not right for Macedonians to be insulted [this way] for they were better men than those who were laughing at them. Alexander retorted that if Cleitus was trying to disguise cowardice as misfortune, he must be pleading his own case. At this, Cleitus sprang to his feet and shouted back: "Yes, it was my cowardice that saved your life, you who call yourself the son of the gods. . . it is the blood of these Macedonians and their wounds which have made you so great that you disown your father Philip and claim to be the son of Ammon!" These words made Alexander furious. "You scum," he cried out, "do you think you can keep on speaking of me like this . . . and not pay for it?" "Oh, but we Macedonians do pay for it," Cleitus retorted. "Just think of the rewards we get for all our efforts. It's the dead ones who are happy because they never lived to see Macedonians being beaten with [Persian] rods, or begging the Persians for an audience with our own king."

As the verbal battle continued, several of the older Macedonians tried to calm the two angry men. But eventually Alexander grabbed a spear from one of his guards. And before anyone could stop him he lurched forward and ran Cleitus through the abdomen. Seeing his friend lying dead, the king suddenly came to his senses. In

Jean Andre Castaigne's
engraving of Alexander
killing Cleitus

a fit of grief he turned the weapon on himself, intending to puncture his own throat. However, his guards restrained him and carried him away to his quarters. For three days he mourned, refusing to eat, shave, or change his clothes.

The unfortunate incident made Alexander more aware than ever of the tensions that had arisen between him and many of his officers. Indeed, some historians think that it was more than his drunken state that had made him lash out. Thanks to Philotus's conspiracy and other similar schemes, an unspoken fear of assassination pervaded the court.

In fact, still another such plot was uncovered not long after Cleitus's tragic end. One of Alexander's royal pages, Hermolaus, made him angry and received a beating with a cane as a punishment. Hermolaus then sought revenge. He enlisted the aid of five other pages, who planned to sneak into the king's quarters and kill him in his sleep. But Alexander attended a party that night and did not return until the next morning. In the days that followed, word about the plot leaked out and made its way to Ptolemy, who immediately informed the king. The pages involved in the conspiracy were arrested, tried, and stoned to death.

Fighting rebels and uncovering assassination plots were not the only activities that occupied Alexander during the three years he spent in Bactria, Sogdiana, and neighboring regions. He also expended considerable time and energy colonizing the region. His men erected many forts and new cities. His strategy was to establish Greek social and cultural bases, as well as military ones, in the lands he conquered. So he settled thousands of Macedonians and other Greeks in the new cities, along with members of the native populations. As might be expected, Greeks and former Persian nobles made up the ruling class, while natives of average or below average means formed the subservient working classes.

Typical of these new settlements was Alexandria Eschate, or Alexandria the Farthest, just south of the Jaxartes River in Sogdiana. Its name "the Farthest" derived from the fact that it was the northernmost and most remote of all the cities Alexander founded. According to Arrian, Alexander viewed the site as "a good one. A settlement there would be likely to increase in size and importance, and would also serve both as an excellent base for a possible future invasion of Scythia and as a defensive position against raiding tribes from across the river."

With these goals in mind, Alexander set thousands of his men to work. And a more than four-mile-long defensive wall, along with hundreds of houses, were completed in only a few weeks. A number of retiring Macedonian veterans immediately moved into these homes.

While establishing forts and towns in the former eastern Persian provinces, Alexander had more in mind than a possible invasion of Scythia. Beyond the far borders of these provinces loomed India. To the Greeks and other Europeans, it had long been a distant and mysterious land situated on the outer edge of the world. To Alexander, it was also his next logical target.

Alexander's men attack an enemy fortress
(Courtesy of Mary Evans Picture Library / Alamy)

Bronze bust of Alexander at Kalithea
Spa on the Island of Rhodes, Greece

CHAPTER EIGHT

INDIA AND THE FAR HORIZON

I n the winter of 327-326 BC, Alexander was twenty-nine years old. Incredibly, he had already established nearly seventy new cities. His empire, stretching from Macedonia through Asia Minor, Palestine, Egypt, Mesopotamia, Iran, and Bactria encompassed more than 1.5 million square miles. And he and his appointed governors ruled more than 100 million people.

Yet apparently this was still not enough to satisfy the young man's thirst for fame, territory, power, and glory. Situated along Bactria's eastern border was the Indus River valley, the traditional border separating the former Persian Empire from the fabled land of India. India was not then a unified country (nor was it ever so in ancient times). Rather, it consisted of many independent, competing kingdoms, some of them extremely well organized, culturally advanced, and militarily strong.

It is unclear how much Alexander knew about India before he entered it. Most likely the information he had was sketchy. Arrian makes the point that one of the major achievements of Alexander's invasion of India was to reveal large amounts of formerly unknown information about that land. Whatever Alexander knew about it beforehand, he certainly did not foresee the ultimate outcome of invading it. In the end, it would prove to be largely a waste of time, lives, and resources and mark the end of his long, phenomenally successful series of conquests.

As he approached the Indus early in 326 BC, however, Alexander was still quite confident of achieving still more military victories and personal glory. In his impulsive fashion, he pushed for a speedy onslaught designed to strike fear into the natives.

His officer Hephaestion traveled ahead with a few thousand men. They erected a pontoon bridge on the Indus river, which was wider and more difficult to traverse than any other rivers the Greeks had before encountered. Arrian describes the building of the structure: "As soon as one vessel is securely moored, another is brought up alongside of it, bows-on to the current. . . . Then timbers are rapidly laid [crossways] from one vessel to the other with planks across them to make the structure rigid. The same process is repeated from vessel to vessel, as many as are needed to complete the bridge." When the bridge was completed, the main army soon passed over it unopposed.

The ruins of one of the thriving cities that Alexander encountered in India.
(*Courtesy of Jon Arnold Images Ltd / Alamy*)

The primary reason that no Indian leaders tried to halt or discourage Alexander's crossing of the Indus was that they had heard about his many successful conquests. And just as Alexander had hoped, most of them were afraid. They agreed that it would be safer and more practical to welcome the Greeks than to oppose them. They therefore greeted Alexander with fanfare and open arms in the city of Taxila, near the Indus's eastern bank. These rulers of the local kingdoms brought him expensive gifts and made alliances with him, hoping to save their lands from being overrun and plundered.

One important Indian leader from the region was conspicuously absent from this summit, however: Porus, king of the realm of Pauravaa. His reasons for shunning the meeting appear to have been twofold. First, he had long been at odds with Taxiles, ruler of Taxila. Also, Porus had made it clear that he was not going to knuckle under to the invaders without a struggle.

Never one to shrink from a fight, Alexander accepted the challenge and led his army toward the Hydaspes River, which marked the western boundary of Porus's kingdom. (Hydaspes is the river's ancient Greek name. The Indians of that era called it the Vitasta and today it is the Jhelum.) Reaching the river, Alexander and his men could see the native army arrayed on a sandy plain on the opposite bank. It must have been an impressive sight. Porus had amassed at least 20,000 and possibly as many as 50,000 infantry; between 2,000 and 4,000 cavalry; more than three-hundred chariots; and about two-hundred battle elephants. (The Indians had pioneered the use of elephants in battle, an approach the Persians and Greeks copied.)

In comparison, Alexander had his usual contingents of Macedonian pikemen, Companion Cavalry, and Greek allies. He also had a few thousand Bactrian fighters (mostly mounted archers) and about 5,000 Indian allies from the Taxila region. His total army was likely not more than 40,000 strong. That this was approximately the same size as his forces in his earlier large pitched battles may not have been a coincidence. Many scholars believe he felt that this number and breakdown of soldiers gave him the most effective blend of power, mobility, and strategic flexibility to defeat the kinds of armies he encountered in Asia.

Because the Hydaspes was wide and deep, Alexander did not charge right across, as he had done at the Granicus. Instead, he bided his time and engaged Porus in a proverbial cat and mouse game. Porus guarded all the major crossing points. Where possible, he stationed his elephants on the riverbank because the huge beasts frightened the Macedonian horses. According to Arrian,

> [Porus] was determined to stop the Macedonians from getting over [the river]. Alexander's answer was by continual movement of his own troops to keep Porus guessing. He split his force into a number of detachments, moving. . . hither and thither all over the place. . . now in this direction, now in that. . . . Every night [Alexander] kept moving the greater part of his mounted troops up and down the bank of the river, making as much noise as possible—shouts, war-cries, and every sort of clatter. . . which might be supposed to precede an attempted crossing.

These troop movements and commotions were mere ploys, however. Porus had his own men and elephants mirror the enemy movements on the other side of the river to make sure that no Greeks tried to make a crossing. As the weeks went by, the seeming stalemate made it look as though Alexander could not and might never find a suitable crossing point. And just as he had anticipated, Porus eventually acquired a false sense of security and let down his guard. One night Alexander left Craterus in charge of several thousand troops in their main camp. This was designed to make it look as if the Greeks had bedded down for the night. However, under the cover of darkness Alexander led the bulk of his troops to an unguarded crossing point eighteen miles to the north. The men maintained strict silence; and the onset of a sudden rainstorm helped to conceal their crossing to the far riverbank.

At first light, the Macedonians and their allies marched southward toward Porus. Alexander placed a force of 1,000 archers in the lead. They were ready to fire a deadly volley of arrows at the Indian elephants if Porus tried to use them to scare his opponents. Meanwhile, the Indian king received word that some enemy soldiers had crossed the river. But seeing that the Greek camp was still occupied, he assumed that the approaching forces were small. So he sent only 2,000 horsemen, commanded by his son, to deal with the threat. This was a serious error. Alexander easily overran the Indian cavalry, killing Porus's son in the process.

Porus did not have time to grieve. Finally realizing that Alexander

PORUS EVENTUALLY ACQUIRED A FALSE SENSE OF SECURITY AND LET DOWN HIS GUARD. ONE NIGHT ALEXANDER LEFT CRATERUS IN CHARGE OF SEVERAL THOUSAND TROOPS IN THEIR MAIN CAMP.

himself was bearing down on him, he hastily organized his soldiers into appropriate battlefield formations. Mere minutes later Alexander arrived and opened the battle, per usual, with a cavalry attack by his right wing. It struck the Indian left wing with devastating force. In response, Porus's own right wing now moved across the plain in hopes of trapping the Macedonian cavalry between the two Indian wings. But Alexander's capable officer Coenus led a large unit of horsemen in an assault on the rear of the Indian right wing. Many of the Indians now fell back, trying to find protection behind their line of elephants.

Porus, too, was relying on his mighty elephants to help turn the tide of battle. At his order to their drivers, the beasts surged forward toward the oncoming Macedonian phalanx. At first, the elephants did some damage, trampling and mangling some of the pikemen in the front ranks. But soon

Alexander's men showered both the beasts and their drivers with javelins and arrows. Bellowing with fear, several of the elephants ran amok, crashing back into the Indian ranks and creating a seething mass of fear and death. As the Indians in the center struggled, the men in the Macedonian phalanx locked shields and charged. Wanting no part of the terrifying forest of pikes, thousands of Porus's soldiers fled. By this time, however, Craterus had crossed the river with his forces and these fresh troops intercepted many of the enemy before they could escape the field.

Porus eventually realized that he had lost the battle. But though he himself had been wounded, he refused to give up. Sitting atop one of his elephants, he challenged the enemy soldiers who had surrounded him. At Alexander's orders, these troops held back and waited. The dramatic stand-

HIS AIR WAS OF **ONE BRAVE MAN** MEETING ANOTHER OF A KING IN THE PRESENCE OF A KING, WITH WHOM HE HAD FOUGHT HONORABLY FOR HIS KINGDOM.

off continued until Alexander sent in an Indian nobleman whom Porus knew well to negotiate an honorable surrender.

After his wounds had been tended to, Porus received a visit from Alexander. The latter much admired his adversary, for unlike Darius, Porus had chosen to fight to the bitter end rather than flee. That the Indian king remained defiant even in captivity also impressed Alexander.

Arrian described the initial meeting between Alexander and his defeated opponent.

An illustration by Jean Andre Castaigne of Porus surrendering to Alexander

> [Alexander] looked at his adversary with admiration. He [Porus] was a magnificent figure of a man. . . and of great personal beauty. His bearing had lost none of its pride. His air was of one brave man meeting another, of a king in the presence of a king, with whom he had fought honorably for his kingdom. Alexander was the first to speak. "What," he said, "do you wish I should do with you?" "Treat me as a king ought [to be treated]," Porus is said to have replied. "For my part," said Alexander, pleased by his answer, "your request shall be granted. But is there not something you would wish for yourself? Ask it." "Everything," said Porus, "is contained in this one request."

Porus could not be sure that he would receive the treatment he had requested. He was not in a position to make demands, after all, since he had been thoroughly and decisively defeated. About 20,000 of his foot soldiers were dead, along with some 3,000 of his horsemen. In addition, all of his chariots had been destroyed and all of his elephants had been either killed or captured. Perhaps worst of all for Porus, two of his sons had fallen in the fighting. In contrast, Alexander had lost only about one-hundred Macedonians and roughly nine hundred Greek, Persian, and Indian allies.

Yet Alexander did not treat Porus as a loser. Instead, he restored the dignified Indian to his throne and made him a trusted ally. Alexander also persuaded Porus to settle his differences with the ruler Taxila. These moves were not motivated merely by generosity or a spirit of good will. Alexander planned to continue eastward in his campaigns, and it was in his best interests to make sure that the conquered peoples in his rear were pacified and cooperative with him and one another. To further strengthen his holdings and supply lines, he built two new towns on the Hydaspes not far from the site of his great victory. One he named Nicaea. The other was called Bucephala, after his beloved horse, which had recently died of old age.

These and other cities in western India were expected to provide Alexander with the supplies he required to conquer the rest of southern Asia. Exactly how long this would take was impossible to say because he and his advisors did not know how big India was. Nor could they be absolutely sure what lay beyond it. The common wisdom among Greeks and other Europeans had long been that a vast circular waterway called the Ocean surrounded the world's land portions. And Alexander may have expected that upon reaching India's far horizon, or easternmost limits, he would gaze on the Ocean's fabled waters.

To reach that distant horizon, however, he first had to conquer several more Indian kingdoms. Of these, the most famous and reportedly the wealthiest and militarily the strongest was Magadha, situated several hundred miles east of the Hydaspes. As usual unafraid of a tough challenge and confident in his own abilities, Alexander looked forward to the new campaign. However, most of his men did not. They were worn out from what seemed a never-ending series of grueling marches and battles. "The sight of their king undertaking an endless succession of dangerous and exhausting enterprises was beginning to depress them," as Arrian described it. And "their enthusiasm was ebbing."

Another problem was that the soldiers had heard rumors about Alexander's new primary goal Magadha. Natives of Porus's realm said that the Magadhan army was far larger and more lethal than their own.

Considering these factors, it is not hard to see why many of Alexander's men finally lost heart. Reaching the Hyphasis River (now the Beas), almost four hundred miles beyond the spot where they had crossed the Indus, they refused to go on. "They held meetings in camp," according to Arrian. "Even the best of them grumbled at their fate, while others swore that they would go no further, not even if Alexander himself led them." Faced with a full-fledged mutiny, although a nonviolent one, Alexander gave the men a long pep talk. But his efforts were futile. Eventually, his trusted deputy Coenus stepped forward and presented the soldiers' side of the argument.

As quoted in Arrian's account, Coenus told Alexander that each of his soldiers:

> longs to see his parents again, if they yet survive, or his wife, or his children. All are yearning for the familiar earth of home, hoping. . . to live to revisit it, no longer in poverty and obscurity, but famous and enriched by the treasure you have enabled them to win. Do not try to lead men who are unwilling to follow you. If their heart is not in it, you will never find the old spirit or the old courage. Consent rather yourself to return to your mother and your home. Once there, you may bring good government to Greece and en-

Jean Andre Castaigne's romanticized illustration of a ladder breaking and stranding Alexander and his companions in the Mallian town

ter your ancestral house with all the glory of the many victories won in this campaign. . . . Sir, if there is one thing above all others a successful man should know, it is when to stop.

Some of the soldiers applauded Coenus, while others were so moved by his words and the courage it took to speak them that they wept. As for Alexander, he was at first resistant. Clearly he wanted to press on and acquire as much territory and glory as he could before his time on earth ran out. At that moment he may have been thinking about his hero Achilles, who, despite his superhuman valor, had died too young. But it quickly became plain to Alexander that his men had made up their minds. And with great reluctance, he agreed to turn back.

Another unpleasant reality that Alexander and his men discovered was that the homeward march would sometimes be almost as difficult and dangerous as the campaigns had been. Indeed, well before they reached the Indus, a local people—the Mallians—amassed a large army and challenged them. Alexander won the battle, and when the surviving Mallians retreated toward one of their fortified cities, he gave chase. He ordered his men to place scaling ladders against the walls and, intoxicated by "the sheer pleasure of battle," in Arrian's words, he joined them in the upward climb.

Suddenly, several of the ladders fell, leaving the king and a handful of his men marooned atop the battlements. Having no where else to go, they descended into the town, where, hugely outnumbered, they fought for their lives. Alexander was wounded by an arrow in the chest. "Despite the pain," Arrian writes, "he continued to defend himself so long as the blood was warm. But. . . overcome by giddiness and faintness he fell forward over his shield." Two of the king's comrades held their own shields up over his body in a desperate effort to protect him. All three would have been killed had the Hypaspists not broken in in the nick of time and saved them. (At the time, the Macedonians thought their leader was dead and in a fit of rage slew every person in the town.)

Alexander swiftly recovered from his wounds. But his brush with death must have reminded him once again that an untimely end could overtake him at any moment.

The wounded Alexander greets some of his troops on the Indus River.
Illustration by Jean Andre Castaigne.

One of several surviving ancient busts of Alexander

CHAPTER NINE

A POWER MORE THAN HUMAN

O nce he had accepted the verdict of his men—that his eastern campaigns were over—Alexander formulated a new set of bold, visionary goals. He decided that the return to Persia, and eventually to Greece, must not be a mere backward march. Instead, he would return by a completely different route, far to the south of the one that had taken him to India. In the process, he would bring new cities and peoples into his vast empire; he would also explore the coasts of what later came to be called the Indian Ocean, paving the way for Greek traders and colonizers.

At the same time, Alexander's mind was racing ahead to the prospect of new grand conquests. The huge Arabian peninsula seemed ripe for the picking. And eventually, he hoped to add all of Europe to his realm, if, that is, he had the time to conquer it. As always, he was haunted by a nagging worry that his tenure on earth might be too short for him to accomplish all the Herculean tasks he dreamed of.

Alexander's most immediate task was to undertake the long and ambitious return trek. To this end, he had a fleet of small ships assembled on the Hydaspes. These vessels carried his army southward until the river merged with the Indus. At a point about half way to the sea, he split his forces n two, sending Craterus and a large portion of the army westward through

SCYTHIANS

Pæonians

ILLYRIA

THRACE

BLACK SEA

MACEDONIA

Pella

Hellespont

Gordium

E. Granicus

Propontis

Corinth

GREECE

LYDIA

Ephesus

Sardis

PHRYGIA

Miletus

Halicarnassus

LYCIA

Taurus Mts.

MEDITERRANEAN SEA

Tarsus

Issus

MESOPOTAMIA

Gaugamela

Arbela

Thapsacus

Tigris

Ec

Sidon

SYRIA

Euphrates R.

Tyre

Babylon

Parætonium

Alexandria

Gaza

BABY

R.

Memphis

ARABIA

Ammon

EGYPT

Nile

EMPIRE OF

ALEXANDE

THE GREAT

(B.C. 323)

RED SEA

Marches of Alexander

Voyage of Nearchus

SCALE OF MILES

200   400   600   800

Map of the empire of Alexander the Great in 323 BC
(Courtesy StockImages/Alamy)

Arachosia and Iran. Alexander and the rest of his followers continued down the Indus to Pattala, in the river's large delta. In the weeks that followed, they explored the region. They also built docks and small naval bases at strategic points in anticipation of creating trade depots for what Alexander expected to be a lively commerce between India and the Mediterranean world.

When the thirty-one-year-old monarch was ready to leave the delta region, he divided his forces a second time. He put his officer Nearchus in charge of the fleet and ordered him to sail along the Indian Ocean's northern coast. Nearchus's main job was to chart the coast and study and record the tides, currents, and wind patterns. Alexander felt that this information would be invaluable to the Greek traders and other mariners who would ply these waters in the future.

Meanwhile, Alexander set out with the rest of his company in a parallel course by land. While incorporating the coastal regions into his empire, he planned to leave stockpiles of food and supplies for Nearchus at intervals along the shore. Unfortunately for all involved, however, Alexander's and Nearchus's groups lost track of each other. Then disaster struck the land forces as they became lost in the arid, barren wastes of Gedrosia (now in southern Pakistan). As described by Arrian, "The blazing heat and the lack of water caused innumerable casualties, especially among the animals, most of which died of thirst. . . . Sometimes they met with lofty hills of sand—loose, deep sand into which they sank as if it were mud."

As the days dragged on, they killed most of the pack animals for food. But the animals were not the only casualties. Many of the women and children following the soldiers died in a sudden flash flood when a cloudburst turned a mountain stream into a deadly torrent. Also, the sick and wounded men had to be abandoned, "for there were no transport animals left." Arrian continued "Even the wagons were being continually broken up as it became more and more impossible to drag them through the deep sand. . . . Many men would fall asleep in their tracks. The few who had strength left to do so followed the army when they woke up again. . . but the greater number perished—poor castaways in the ocean of sand."

Eventually, Alexander and the survivors of his party established contact with Craterus in Carmania (now in southeastern Iran). Craterus gave his suffering countrymen pack animals and supplies, making it possible for them to go on. Delighted, Alexander "offered sacrifice in gratitude to heaven

This modern photo shows part of the bleak, arid wilderness through which
Alexander and his army marched on their arduous return trek.
(Courtesy Fabienne Fossez / Alamy)

for [the] escape of his army from the desert of Gedrosia," Arrian wrote. Alexander also celebrated by holding "a festival with public competitions in
athletics and the arts."

In addition, Alexander caught up with Nearchus near the entrance
to the Persian Gulf. At first, the king assumed that all the ships had been lost
and that Nearchus and the handful of men accompanying him were the sole
survivors. Then the admiral informed him that most of the ships and their
crews were safe. At this, Alexander burst into tears of joy. A few days later
the land and sea parties continued their separate journeys until they met up
again at Susa in the spring of 324 BC.

From Susa, Alexander made his way back to Babylon, where jubilant crowds welcomed him and his soldiers. The king was disappointed to

Alexander's second entrance into Babylon was not as lavish as the first one, as depicted in Le Brun's famous painting. *(Courtesy StockImages/Alamy)*

find that there had been a considerable amount of political corruption in the region in his absence. Particularly upsetting was the news that an old Macedonian friend, Harpalus, whom he had earlier made a high-ranking financial officer, was one of the main culprits. Hearing of Alexander's approach, Harpalus had fled back to Greece. There he used some of the money he had embezzled to bribe the Athenians into giving him shelter. But they soon ordered his arrest. Escaping, he went to Crete, where some of his own deputies slew him in hopes of avoiding Alexander's wrath.

While dealing with those guilty of misconduct, Alexander turned to the tasks of managing his empire and planning for its eventual expansion. First, he made Babylon his imperial capital. This move may have been motivated by practicality. Babylon was located about halfway between central Europe and India. Parts of the latter were already under his control, and he anticipated that Europe, too, would eventually be his. In fact, during his stay in Babylon he received ambassadors from several leading European and north African kingdoms and regions, including Libya, Carthage, Italy, Spain, and Gaul (what is now France). The leaders of these places had heard that the conqueror of Asia had returned. And they likely felt that they should try to get on his good side before he decided to attack them next.

Alexander's more immediate plans included the large-scale colonization of the Persian Gulf region and an invasion of Arabia. Both of these immense projects required large numbers of ships. And to that end he instituted a huge ship-building program. According to Arrian, in addition to Nearchus's fleet,

> Alexander was having a new flotilla built as well, and for this purpose was felling the cypresses in Babylonia. . . . Manpower and crews for the new vessels were supplied by shell-divers and others whose work was connected with the sea, from Phoenicia and the neighboring seaboard. He also. . . began the construction of a harbor at Babylon large enough for 1,000 warships to lie in, and equipped with [dock]yards. . . . The fact is, Alexander had ideas of settling the seaboard of the Persian Gulf and the off-shore islands; for he fancied it might become as prosperous a country as Phoenicia. The naval preparations were directed against the Arabs of the coast. . . . Arabia, too, was a large country, its coast. . .

no less in extent than the coast of India. Many islands lay off it, and there were harbors everywhere fit for his fleet to rise in and to provide sites for new settlements likely to grow to great wealth and prosperity.

None of these far-reaching enterprises ever came to fruition, however. Alexander's longstanding fears of dying before his time finally proved warranted, for on or about June 10, 323 BC he died in his palace in Babylon. In a month or two he would have been thirty-three. His ancient biographers offered detailed accounts of his last hours. Plutarch's version says that on June 2 Alexander slept in the bathing room because he was feverish. The next evening he bathed, offered a sacrifice to the gods, and dined. Through that night and the next day his fever remained high. In the days that followed his senior commanders remained on call in the courtyard of the palace at Alexander's orders. His fever continued, and he was unable to speak when his commanders entered his room and filed past his bedside. On June 10, or by some accounts the next evening, he died.

In this nineteenth-century illustration by Karl Von Piloty, soldiers pay tribute to a dying Alexander. *(Courtesy of North Wind Picture Archives/Alamy).*

The exact cause of Alexander's death remains unknown. Both ancient and modern scholars have ventured theories and guesses. One is that one or more of his closer followers poisoned him. It has also been suggested that the bouts of fever mentioned in several ancient accounts were a symptom of malaria, which he might have contracted in his travels in southern Asia. More recently, a convincing case has been made that he died of alcohol poisoning. This would not be surprising, considering the many ancient descriptions of him drinking himself into a stupor.

One of the more compelling theories for Alexander's untimely death is that of University of Louisville scholar Robert B. Kebric, who writes:

> That the most immediate cause of Alexander's death as described by Arrian and Plutarch appears to have been alcohol poisoning can hardly be a surprising revelation, since it was a common occurrence in antiquity and not infrequent within Alexander's own experience. Strong evidence concerning the death of Alexander's closest friend, Hephaestion, indicates that it was the result of heavy drinking. Elsewhere, it is written that after the death of another valued friend. . . Alexander proposed a drinking contest in which forty-two of the competitors, including the victor, died from consuming too much [wine]. . . . When the medical details included as part of Arrian's and Plutarch's accounts of Alexander's death are compared with specific unrelated cases in the corpus [writings] of [the famous Greek physician] Hippocrates, the most convincing immediate reason that emerges for Alexander's death is that he did ultimately die from the effects of alcohol poisoning.

Whatever killed Alexander, his legacy was too huge to die with him. His conquests and political policies had changed much of the known world permanently and in far-reaching ways. First, his leading generals and governors could not agree on who should succeed him. So they, and some of their sons, fought one another in a series of devastating battles and wars lasting nearly forty years. Chief among these so-called Diadochoi, or Successors, were Antipater, Craterus, Perdiccas, Antigonus, Ptolemy, Seleucus, Eumenes, Lysimachus, Cassander (Antipater's son), Demetrius Poliorcetes (Antigonus's son), and Antigonus Gonatas (Demetrius's son and Antigonus's grandson).

The overall result of these struggles was the breakup of Alexander's enormous empire into several large, Greek-ruled kingdoms. The principal ones were the Ptolemaic Kingdom (consisting of Egypt and parts of Palestine), founded by Ptolemy; the Seleucid Kingdom (centered in Mesopotamia), established by Seleucus; and the Macedonian Kingdom (made up of Macedonia and most of mainland Greece), founded by Antigonus Gonatas.

For three centuries, these powerful empires, along with other surviving Greek states, controlled what modern historians call the Hellenistic world. The term *Hellenistic* means "Greek-like." It refers to the long-lasting imposition of Greek politics and culture over those of the non-Greeks Alexander had conquered. Only when the Romans and Parthians (an Asian people) defeated the Successor kingdoms did the Hellenistic Age (323-30 BC) end, and with it the last major vestiges of Greek political power in the ancient world. (Even then, Greek ideas and artistic styles remained influential in many parts of southern and western Asia, as well as in Europe, for centuries to come.)

Another important aspect of Alexander's legacy was the larger-than-life image of him that posterity inherited. In life, he was far from perfect. Indeed, he had many faults, including arrogance, impatience, recklessness, and at times cruelty. Yet he displayed enormous talent and drive, carved out the largest empire the world had yet seen, and, for good or ill, affected the lives of millions of people, all in little more than a decade.

For these reasons, later generations saw Alexander as somehow superhuman; hence they came to call him "the Great." Arrian ably sums up why that lofty title seemed appropriate in his own day and remains no less fitting more than two millennia later:

> He had great personal beauty, invincible power of endurance, and a keen intellect [and] an uncanny instinct for the right course in a difficult and complex situation. . . . Noble indeed was his power of inspiring his men, of filling them with confidence [and] sweeping away their fear by the spectacle of his own fearlessness. . . . There was in those days no nation, no city, no single individual beyond the reach of Alexander's name. Never in all the world was there another like him, and therefore I cannot but feel that some power more than human was concerned in his birth, [and] there is the further evidence of the extraordinary way in which he is held, as no mere man could be, in honor and remembrance.

THE PTOLEMIES IN EGYPT

One of the major outcomes of Alexander's conquests was the takeover of Egypt by his longtime deputy and friend Ptolemy. The result was a Greek dynasty (family line of rulers) that controlled that nation and surrounding regions for nearly three centuries. Alexander and Ptolemy knew each other as young Macedonian nobles. And Ptolemy served loyally and effectively on the other man's general staff in Persia and the other lands that Alexander overran.

After Alexander's death in 323 BC, Ptolemy became one of the so-called Successors, who together agreed that he would rule Egypt. After taking charge of that country, Ptolemy also seized Alexander's body while it was being transported back to Greece from Babylon. Having control of the dead conqueror's remains made Ptolemy the most important Successor in the eyes of many Greeks.

At first, Ptolemy governed Egypt in Alexander's name. But eventually he declared himself pharaoh (the Egyptian name for king) and ruled as an absolute monarch. His official title became Ptolemy I Soter ("Savior"). And his domains included parts of Palestine and Asia Minor, as well as Egypt itself. Many Greek merchants, soldiers, and administrators migrated to Egypt during his reign. With his help, they formed a privileged social class who treated most native Egyptians as inferiors. Ptolemy also turned Alexandria into a magnificent cultural center. He began work on the famous Great Library, which eventually held tens of thousands of manuscripts.

Ptolemy died in 283 BC. Most of his successors in the Ptolemaic dynasty were less talented and effective on the throne than he had been. One major exception was the last of the Ptolemies—Cleopatra VII (69-30 BC). A shrewd, ambitious ruler, she allied herself with two powerful Romans—Julius Caesar and Mark Antony. With the latter, she made a daring bid for world domination before suffering defeat at the hands of a third Roman power broker, Octavian. (Soon afterward he became Augustus, the first Roman emperor.) The former Ptolemaic Empire then became a Roman province.

The Library of Alexandria housed more than a half million documents from Assyria, Greece, Persia, India, Egypt, and other nations. More than one hundred scholars also lived there, conducting research, writing, lecturing, or translating and copying documents. Construction began under Ptolemy I (305-285 BC) and continued under Ptolemy II (285-246 BC). Ptolemy II is credited with the idea of asking rulers of other states to contribute books.
(Courtesy of North Wind Picture Archives/Alamy).

الإسكندر الأكبر

٣٥٦ - ٣٢٣ ق.م.

ALEXANDER
THE
GREAT
(356 BC – 323 BC)

A statute of Alexander the Great stands near the New Library of Alexandria, in Egypt. The New Library (now called Bibliotheca Alexandrina) is about one hundred yards from where the ancient library stood.
(Courtesy of Gary Cook/Alamy).

TIMELINE

480: Persia's King Xerxes invades Greece; driven away by coalition of city-states.

413-399: Reign of Macedonian king Archelaus I, who establishes new capital at Pella.

359: King Philip II assumes power in Macedonia.

357: Philip marries Olympias, a princess of the small kingdom of Epirus.

356: Alexander is born in Pella to Philip and Olympias.

343: Tutored by renowned Athenian scholar Aristotle.

340: Serves as Macedonia's regent while Philip is away; puts down a rebellion and founds a new town.

338: With Philip, defeats an alliance of southern city-states at Chaeronea, near Thebes.

337: Philip announces plans to invade the Persian Empire.

336: Becomes King of Macedonia after Philip is assassinated.

335: Puts down rebellions in Thrace and Illyria; destroys city of Thebes after it rebels.

334: Invades Persia, crossing the Hellespont into Asia Minor; at the Granicus River, defeats an army commanded by several local Persian governors.

333: At Gordium, in central Asia Minor, unravels the Gordium knot, fulfilling a prophecy; defeats Persia's King Darius III at Issus.

331: Establishes a new city in the Nile Delta, naming it Alexandria; defeats Darius again at Gaugamela.

330: Captures Persian capital of Persepolis and burns its palaces; pursues Darius; executes officers Philotus and Parmenio for plotting against him.

329: Captures Bessus, Darius's murderer.

328: Kills his close friend and general Cleitus in a drunken rage.

326: Defeats Indian king Porus on the Hydaspes River; troops refuse to go any farther into India and demand to return home. Bucephalas dies.

325: Begins return journey.

324: Makes Babylon the capital of empire; begins planning the invasion of Arabia.

323: Dies in Babylon at the age of thirty-two.

323-30: The Hellenistic Age; Alexander's leading generals and governors, the Successors, fight one another for possession of his empire, which is carved up into large Greek-controlled kingdoms; these states fight among themselves until they are attacked and defeated by the increasingly powerful Romans and Parthians.

GLOSSARY

antiquity — Ancient times.

archenemy — A traditional foe.

cavalry — Mounted soldiers.

confederation — An alliance of independent political states.

dekadarch — The commander of a dekas.

dekas — In the Macedonian phalanx, a single file of sixteen men.

Diadochoi — The Successors, or Alexander's leading generals and governors,who fought for control of his empire after his death.

dynasty — A family line of rulers.

flanks — The sides of a military formation.

hegemon — In ancient Greece, a supreme leader.

Hellenistic — "Greek-like," a reference to the Successor kingdoms and the era in which they dominated the Greek world.

Herculean — Extremely difficult and daunting, like the feats of the mythical Greek strongman Heracles (now better known as Hercules).

hetairoi — "Companion cavalry"; the principal cavalry unit in the army of Philip II and his son, Alexander the Great.

hoplite — In ancient Greece, a heavily armored infantry soldier.

ilai (singular is ile) — Squadrons of Macedonian cavalry.

infantry — Foot soldiers.

kausia — A beret-like cap worn in ancient Macedonia.

lochos (plural is lochoi) — In a Greek phalanx, a company; in the Macedonian phalanx, it usually numbered about 500 men.

logistics — In warfare, the management of the flow of supplies.

lyre — A small harp.

mercenary — A hired soldier.

outflank — To move around and behind the opposing troops in a battle.

pachyderm — An elephant.

pezhetairoi — "Foot-companions"; the name Macedonia's King Philip II gave to the members of his phalanx.

phalanx — A Greek military formation consisting of multiple ranks, with soldiers standing, marching, or fighting side by side in each rank.

predestination — The notion that a god or fate sometimes bestows special powers or destinies on chosen humans.

prophecy — A prediction of future events.

proskynesis — The Persian custom of prostrating oneself before a king.

sap — A tunnel dug beneath an enemy's walls during a siege.

sarissa — A long pike wielded by members of the Macedonian phalanx.

satrap — The governor of a satrapy.

satrapy — A province of the Persian Empire.

shock action — Direct attacks by cavalry on infantry.

siege tower — A tall wooden structure, usually mounted on wheels, employed in ancient sieges; archers and other soldiers usually rode inside the tower as it came up alongside the enemy's walls.

synedrion — In ancient Greece, a large-scale meeting or conference.

taxis (plural is taxeis) — In ancient Greek armies, a brigade or battalion; in the Macedonian phalanx it usually numbered about 1,500 men.

xyston — A spear or lance wielded by ancient Greek cavalrymen.

Sources

Chapter One: The World of Alexander's Boyhood

P. 6, "Those who endure hardship . . ." Arrian, *Anabasis Alexandri* 5.26. trans. Don Nardo.

P. 7, "The bride dreamed . . ." Plutarch, *Life of Alexander, in The Age of Alexander: Nine Greek Lives* by Plutarch, trans. Ian Scott-Kilvert (New York: Penguin, 1973), 253.

P. 12, "built up their morale . . ." Diodorus Siculus, Library of History Cambridge, MA: Harvard University Press, 1962-1967), vol. 7, 241.

P. 13, "Philip found you a tribe . . ." Quoted in Arrian, Anabasis Alexandri, published as *The Campaigns of Alexander,* trans. Aubrey de Sélincourt (New York: Penguin, 1986), 360-361.

P. 13, "He was fair-skinned . . ." Plutarch, *Life of Alexander,* 255.

P. 15, "considered the task . . ." Ibid., 258.

P. 14, "He regarded the Iliad . . ." Ibid., 259-260.

P. 16, "He was wild . . ." Ibid., 257-258.

P. 14, "Whenever he heard . . ." Ibid., 256.

P. 17, "Philip became extravagantly fond . . ." Ibid., 261.

Chapter Two: In Philip's Mighty Shadow

P. 23, "There are a number . . ." Polybius, *Histories,* published as *Polybius: The Rise of the Roman Empire,* Trans. Ian Scott-Kilvert, (New York: Penguin, 1980), 509-510.

P. 24, "good and bad . . ." Plutarch, *Moralia: Apophthegms,* or *Sayings of Kings and Commanders,* http://www.bostonleadershipbuilders.com/plutarch/moralia/sayings_of_kings.htm

P. 26, "He cannot rest content . . ." Demosthenes, *First Philippic, in Demosthenes, Olynthiacs, Philippics, Minor Speeches,* Trans. J.H. Vince (Cambridge, MA: Harvard University Press, 1998), 73, 75.

P. 26, "The news stunned the Athenians . . ." Plutarch, *Life of Demosthenes, in The Age of Alexander,* 203.

P. 26, "If anyone imagines . . ." Demosthenes, *Second Philippic, in Demosthenes, Olynthiacs, Philippics, Minor Speeches,* 127, 133, 135.

P. 29, "Let's drive them back . . ." Polyaenus, *Stratagems,* quoted in Peter Green, *Alexander of Macedon, 356-323 B.C.: A Historical Biography* (Berkeley: University of California Press, 1992), 75.

P. 29, "Alexander, his heart set . . ." Diodorus, *Library of History,* vol. 8, 79.

P. 30, "[The unit] consisted of . . ." Plutarch, *Life of Pelopidas, in The Age of Alexander,* 85-86.

Chapter Three: A Brash New Macedonian King

P. 35, "I swear by Zeus . . ." Quoted in "The Corinthian League," http://www.livius.org/aj-al/alexander/alexander_t43.html

P. 36, "Perhaps there are those . . ." Isocrates, Address to Philip, in Kenneth J. Atchity, ed., *The Classical Greek Reader* (New York: Oxford University Press, 1998), 183-184.

P. 37, "Attalus, who had drunk too much . . ." Plutarch, *Life of Alexander,* 261.

P. 38, "Philip appeared . . ." Diodorus, *Library of History,* vol. 8, 95, 99, 101.

P. 40, "They had collected a . . ." Arrian, *Anabasis Alexandri,* 43-44.

P. 41, "As far as the population . . ." Plutarch, *Life of Alexander,* 264.

P. 41, "I am the sister of Theagenes . . ." Ibid., 265.

P. 42, "If it was peace . . ." Plutarch, Life of Phocion, in The Age of Alexander, 232-233.

Chapter Four: Assault on the Greatest Empire

P. 45, "received Asia from the gods . . ." Diodorus, *Library of History,* vol. 8, 163.

P. 50, "There was a profound hush . . ." Arrian, *Anabasis Alexandri,* 72-73.

P. 52, "Alexander quickly had them . . ." Ibid., 75.

P. XX, "To Alexander the strategy of war . . ." Victor D. Hanson, *The Wars of the Ancient Greeks* (New York: HarperCollins, 2006), 176.

P. 53, "Alexander, son of Philip . . ." Quoted in Arrian, *Anabasis Alexandri,* 76.

P. 54, "The catapults mounted on towers . . ." Ibid., 88.

P. 55, "when he and his attendants left . . ." Ibid., 105.

Chapter Five: From Destroyer to Liberator

P. 57, "The Persian cavalry would ride . . ." Arrian, *Anabasis Alexandri,* 110.

P. 58, "We of Macedon . . ." Ibid., 112.

P. 59, "The Persian left collapsed . . ." Ibid., 118-119.

P. 60, "Alexander has sent . . ." Ibid., 126.

P. 61, "Your ancestors invaded . . ." Ibid., 127-128.

P. 63, "On the battlements . . ." Ibid., 137-138.

P. 64, "The main body of the Tyrian defenders . . ." Ibid., 142.

P. 65, "was destined to rule . . ." Plutarch, *Life of Alexander,* 283.

P. 66, "When he saw . . ." Ibid., 282.

P. 67, "There was no chalk . . ." Ibid., 282.

Chapter Six: To Be Master of All Asia

P. 70, "Once over the river . . ." Arrian, *Anabasis Alexandri,* 159.

P. 70, "[The crossing] was accomplished . . ." Diodorus, *Library of History,* vol. 8, 177, 179.

P. 72, "He called upon [the gods] . . ." Quintus Curtius Rufus, *The History of Alexander,* Trans. John Yardley (New York: Penguin, 1984), 80.

P. 72, "The phalanx joined shields . . ." Diodorus, *Library of History*, vol. 8, 285.

P. 73, "Darius was a tall and . . ." Plutarch, *Life of Alexander,* 291.

P. 74, "It was every man for himself . . ." Arrian, *Anabasis Alexandri,* 170-171.

P. 74, "A large number of Babylonians . . ." Curtius, *The History of Alexander,* 93-94.

P. 77, "The Macedonians were all around them . . ." Arrian, *Anabasis Alexandri,* 178.

P. 79, "This is the final stroke . . ." Plutarch, *Life of Alexander,* 300.

Chapter Seven: Adventures in Afghanistan

P. 82, "played a great part . . ." Plutarch, *Life of Alexander,* 303-304.

P. 82, "I beg you, Alexander . . ." Arrian, *Anabasis Alexandri,* 221.

P. 84, "For my part . . ." Ibid., 219-220.

P. 85, "The persons who had reported . . ." Ibid., 191.

P. 85, "The reason for Parmenio's execution . . ." Ibid., 192.

P. 87, "had the tops of two straight trees . . ." Plutarch, *Life of Alexander,* 301.

P. 87, "He [Spitamenes] dispatched . . ." Arrian, *Anabasis Alexandri,* 209-210.

P. 89, "[Cleitus] shouted . . ." Plutarch, *Life of Alexander,* 308.

P. 90, "a good one . . ." Arrian, *Anabasis Alexandri,* 201.

Chapter Eight: India and the Far Horizon

P. 94, "As soon as one vessel . . ." Arrian, *Anabasis Alexandri,* 265.

P. 96, "was determined to stop the Greeks . . ." Ibid., 267, 269.

P. XX, "As a king." Ibid., 281.

P. 100, "[Alexander] looked at his adversary . . ." Ibid., 281.

P. 101, "The sight of their king . . ." Ibid., 291.

P. 101, "They held meetings . . ." Ibid., 291-292.

P. 101, "longs to see his parents again . . ." Ibid., 296-297.

P. 102, "the sheer pleasure of battle . . ." Ibid., 319.

P. 103, "Despite the pain . . ." Ibid., 314.

Chapter Nine: A Power More than Human

P. 108, "The blazing heat . . ." Arrian, *Anabasis Alexandri,* 336-337.

P. 108, "offered sacrifice in gratitude . . ." Ibid., 343.

P. 111, "Alexander was having a new flotilla built . . ." Ibid., 381-383.

P. , "[On June 2] he slept in the bathroom . . ." Plutarch, *Life of Alexander,* 332-333.

P. 113, "The most immediate cause . . ." Robert B. Kebric, "The Death of Alexander the Great: Alcohol Poisoning and Some Case Studies form Hippocrates," Third Annual Hawaii International Conference on Arts and Humanities, Honolulu, HI, January 16, 2005, 4, 13.

P. 115, "He had great personal beauty . . ." ." Arrian, *Anabasis Alexandri,* 395-396, 398.

BIBLIOGRAPHY

Arrian. *Anabasis Alexandri,* published as The Campaigns of Alexander. Trans. Aubrey de Sélincourt. New York: Penguin, 1986.

Atchity, Kenneth J., ed. *The Classical Greek Reader.* New York: Oxford University Press, 1998.

Austin, M.M., ed. *The Hellenistic World from Alexander to the Roman.*

Conquest: A Selection of Ancient Sources in Translation. Cambridge: Cambridge University Press, 2006.

Bosworth, A.B. *Conquest and Empire: The Reign of Alexander the Great.* New York: Cambridge University Press, 1993.

Cartledge, Paul. *Alexander the Great: A New Life.* New York: Overlook, 2005.

Demosthenes. *Olynthiacs, Philippics, Minor Speeches.* Trans. J.H. Vince. Cambridge, MA: Harvard University Press, 1998.

Diodorus Siculus. *Library of History.* 12 vols. Various trans. Cambridge, MA: Harvard University Press, 1962-1967.

Engels, Donald W. *Alexander the Great and the Logistics of the Macedonian Army.* Berkeley: University of California Press, 1980.

Everson, Tim. *Warfare in Ancient Greece.* Stroud, UK: Sutton, 2004.

Fox, Robin Lane. *Alexander the Great.* New York: Penguin, 2004.

Fuller, J. F. C. *The Generalship of Alexander the Great.* Cambridge, MA: Da Capo, 2004.

Green, Peter. *Alexander of Macedon, 356-323 B.C.: A Historical Biography.* Berkeley: University of California Press, 1992.

Hammond, N. G. L. *The Genius of Alexander the Great.* Chapel Hill: University of North Carolina Press, 1998.

———. and G.T. Griffith. *A History of Macedonia, vol. 2.* Oxford: Clarendon Press, 1979.

Hanson, Victor D. *The Wars of the Ancient Greeks.* New York: HarperCollins, 2006.

Hatzopoulos, Miltiades B. and Louisa D. Loukopoulos, eds. *Philip of Macedon.* Athens: Ekdotike Athenon, 1980.

Heckel, Waldemar. *The Wars of Alexander the Great.* London: Osprey, 2007.

Polybius, Histories, published as *Polybius: The Rise of the Roman Empire.* Trans. Ian Scott-Kilvert. New York: Penguin, 1980.

Plutarch. *Moralia: Apophthegms, or Sayings of Kings and Commanders.* http://www.bostonleadershipbuilders.com/plutarch/moralia/sayings_of_kings.htm.

———. Parallel Lives, excerpted in *The Age of Alexander: Nine Greek Lives by Plutarch.* Trans. Ian Scott-Kilvert. New York: Penguin, 1973.

Quintus Curtius Rufus. *The History of Alexander.* Trans. John Yardley. New York: Penguin, 1984.

Rogers, Guy M. *Alexander: The Ambiguity of Greatness.* New York: Random House, 2005.

Sekunda, Nick and John Warry. *Alexander the Great: His Armies and Campaigns, 334-323 B.C.* London: Osprey, 1998.

"The Corinthian League." http://www.livius.org/aj-al/alexander/alexander_t43.html.

Thompson, Michael. *Granicus, 334 B.C.: Alexander's First Persian Victory.* London: Osprey, 2007.

WEB SITES

Alexander the Great

http://www.livius.org/aj-al/alexander/alexander00.html

Part of the "Livius Articles on the Ancient World" online project, this is an excellent general source for Alexander, covering his life, exploits, associates, and enemies, and featuring numerous related links.

Arrian of Nicomedia

http://www.livius.org/arl-arz/arrian/arrian.html

An brief but illuminating look at Alexander's chief ancient biographer, Arrian, with several links to excerpts from his works.

Battle of Gaugamela

http://www.mlahanas.de/Greeks/History/Battles/Gaugamela.html

A handy online reference on one of Alexander's crucial battles, with clear diagrams tracing the various Greek and Persian units and their movements during the conflict.

Battle of Hydaspes

http://joseph_berrigan.tripod.com/ancientbabylon/id36.html

This short but informative synopsis of the biggest battle Alexander fought in India features many colorful graphics.

The Macedonian Army

http://members.tripod.com/~S_van_Dorst/Alexander.html#macarmy

A useful overview of the army, including its command structure. There is also a link to a helpful site containing a list of Greek military terms.

Philip II of Macedonia

http://www.livius.org/phi-php/philip/philip_ii.htm

A good, concise look at Alexander's father and military mentor.

Siege of Tyre

http://joseph_berrigan.tripod.com/ancientbabylon/id34.html

This concise overview of Alexander's most famous siege contains numerous maps, photos, and colorful restorations of the event.

INDEX